MYSTERIOUS BRITISH COLUMBIA

Myths, Murders, Mysteries and Legends

Valerie Green

QUAGMIRE PRESS

© 2011 by Quagmire Press Ltd.
First printed in 2011 10 9 8 7 6 5 4 3 2 1
Printed in Canada

The Publisher: Quagmire Press Ltd.
Website: www.quagmirepress.com

Library and Archives Canada Cataloguing in Publication

Green, Valerie, 1940–
    Mysterious British Columbia / Valerie Green.
Includes bibliographical references.

ISBN 978-1-926695-18-1

    1. Curiosities and wonders—British Columbia. 2. Legends—British Columbia. 3. British Columbia—History—Miscellanea. I. Title.

AG243.G83 2011   001.9409711   C2011-906233-X

Project Director: Hank Boer
Project Editor: Kathy van Denderen
Photo Credits: Every effort has been made to accurately credit the sources of photographs. Any errors or omissions should be reported directly to the publisher for correction in future editions. Photographs courtesy of City of Vancouver Archives (p. 135); Matt Green (pp. 152, 161–163); *Chambers Encyclopedia*, William & Robert Chambers, Limited, ©1899 (p. 223); Royal BC Museum, BC Archives (B-03945, p. 75; A-02986, p. 204); University of Washington Libraries, Special Collections (NOW049, p. 145); Valerie Green (pp. 19, 129, 131, 159).
Cover Images: © Photos.com

Produced with the assistance of the Government of Alberta, Alberta Multimedia Development Fund.

Government of Alberta ■

*I love to **lose myself in a Mystery**...*

–Sir Thomas Browne (1605–82),
Religio Medici, part 1, section 9 (published 1643)

Contents

THE MYSTERIES   125

THE PARANORMAL AND THE LEGENDS   174

Dedication

For Matt and Kate, with love and pride—my two greatest accomplishments in life who continue to amaze me with their talents, abilities and loving ways

Acknowledgements

~

In writing about these unsolved mysteries and crimes, I have tried to be respectful of the families and loved ones of those involved. I acknowledge them all, past and present, with gratitude and with sympathy for the tragedies they have suffered.

I would also like to thank Hank Boer, who saw the potential of these intriguing stories and allowed me the space to add and improve on them. And sincere thanks to Kathy van Denderen for her thorough edit.

I also acknowledge the services of the many archives and organizations I used in my research, including the Royal BC Museum Archives, the Victoria Police Archives, the Saanich Police Department, the Victoria Police Department, the University of Victoria Archives, the University of BC Archives and the Saanich Archives. And thanks to all those individuals who supplied photographic material and to the many people I spoke with about these murders and mysteries throughout the years. Other organizations and websites have been acknowledged with gratitude in the sources at the end of this book.

Thanks also to Evelyn Reitmeyer for acknowledging my emails with graciousness and courtesy, and special thanks to Crystal Dunahee for confirming facts and allowing me the privilege of sharing her family's tragic story.

While working on the William Robinson chapter, I was also grateful for the excellent Canadian Mysteries website, which is a first-rate resource for the amateur detective.

Thanks as always go to my family for their constant support and understanding. Lastly, a very special thank you to my late mother, who always enjoyed reading about a mystery or an unsolved crime and kept numerous newspaper clippings throughout the years, many of which proved invaluable in my research for this book.

Introduction

~

In 1871, with a population of only 36,000, British Columbia became Canada's sixth province. The *British Colonist* newspaper at that time stated, "Today British Columbia and Canada joined hands across the Rocky Mountains…standing with one foot on the Atlantic and the other on the Pacific."

Originally known as New Caledonia, the province's name had been changed to British Columbia by Queen Victoria with Royal Assent back on August 2, 1858. The name chosen for the new province did not, however, immediately meet with everyone's approval. The Queen most probably chose the name "British Columbia" because of the Columbia River running through the area, which in turn had been named for the ship *Columbia,* a vessel that played a large role in the substantial Pacific sea otter trade of the 1780s and 1790s. The name "Columbia" was also the only name at that time that had been given to the surrounding territory on every map the Queen had consulted. So she simply added the word "British," and the name stuck and British Columbia was born. In 1871, the Queen's choice became official when British Columbia joined Confederation.

Today, 140 years later, the province can reflect with pride upon all the early years of challenge placed upon the many gallant pioneering ancestors of yesteryear: the spirited fur traders, miners, farmers, fishermen, loggers and politicians who all contributed in some way to laying the foundation of this great and varied province.

In looking back at BC's history, much of the population in the late 1800s still depended on the declining gold rush to make a substantial living. It was high time for the introduction of new industries. Better communication and transportation were vital if BC was to expand. Until that point, only the stagecoach, the wagon, the pack train or the steamboat connected this most westerly part of Canada to the outside world. It took at least three weeks for a traveller from BC to reach places in the east, and the journey started by steamer from Victoria to San Francisco and then by train across the United States. The need for a Canadian railway became of the utmost importance.

Other industries were also necessary to enhance the growth of the young province—forestry, fishing, manufacturing, mining and farming—but each industry was dependent upon a railway being built. When construction of the railway finally began in 1880, the forestry industry took off as the demand for lumber exploded with the need for railway ties and bridges. Following on the success of forestry came the fishing industry, and with the invention of the tin can, the first fish cannery was built in New Westminster. By the turn of the century, entrepreneurs were making a great deal of money, and fishing and lumber barons were commonplace in the population. BC salmon was known internationally, and the province was finally on the world map.

There is another aspect of the province's history that is noteworthy, but for other reasons, and that is the incredible number of unsolved crimes, mysteries and legends connected to BC. The collection gathered in this book is only a sample of the unsolved mysteries that continue to intrigue and puzzle us.

Included in this chosen selection are some unsolved murder cases, beginning with a Victoria police constable killed in the line of duty in 1859; a black settler on Salt Spring Island killed in 1869; a gruesome series of murders at the Mile 108 Hotel in the Cariboo in the 1870s; a missing family friend accused of a brutal murder in 1898; a Victoria woman who was brutally murdered by an unknown assailant on her way home from work in 1899; and a Scottish nanny in Vancouver, initially thought to have committed suicide in 1923, until evidence proved otherwise. In addition, the story is told of a train disaster near Castlegar that killed a distinguished Doukhobor leader. Completing this collection of murderous crimes are those of Molly Justice in 1943, Marguerite Telesford in 1989 and the murder of a young female real estate agent in 2008, plus two decades of murders and disappearances of young women along Highway 16 in northern BC.

And then there are the mysteries. There is the tale of a Chinese cemetery that never really existed because of a long-ago racial slight; the true story of a miracle birth in 1912 at the once notorious Wigwam Inn on Indian Arm and a few marine mysteries on BC's west coast. Another mystery concerns some unexplainable changes to a painting in Chilliwack as well as the tragic story of a four-year-old boy who disappeared without a trace more than 20 years ago.

In the paranormal and legends section of the book, I've included stories of unfathomable monster sightings, plus anecdotes of the renowned Sasquatch as well as some UFO sightings to ponder upon. And surely no book would be complete without the necessary accounts of at least a few hauntings and some folklore. There is also the intriguing story of the Cariboo camels experiment, one of the more nebulous tales in BC's history.

Finally, a First Nations Christmas legend is told that explores the strong human spirit always apparent when people gather together in a common cause for good.

The stories in this eclectic assortment are true or are legends passed down from generation to generation. Some, such as the chapter on William Robinson, form part of the Great Canadian Mysteries website, offering opportunities for the layperson to try to solve the case. Many of these cases have, naturally, become cold over time, so there may never be an answer to the mystery.

Despite BC's past, or maybe because of it, the mountain ranges that separate this province from the rest of Canada have also in many ways isolated it; it's a province that still tends to look more toward the Pacific than to the Atlantic. However, this very isolation has created a uniqueness of character of the people who live in British Columbia.

Perhaps it's because of this effective progress and independence of character that so many stories of unsolved mysteries, legends and paranormal events have been generated and harvested throughout the years.

This book has been written in an attempt to resurrect and, perhaps even to find a solution, to some of these unsolved BC mysteries.

THE MURDERS

Many of the crimes described in the first section of this book remain part of British Columbia's cold case file history, beginning with the very earliest murders in the 1850s and 1860s. Other murders, although they might well have been officially solved, are still surrounded by mystery and unanswered questions.

As we wander back over the last few decades, from the first unexplained, motive-less murder of a police constable simply doing his duty on the outskirts of Fort Victoria in 1859, down to the brutal slaying of a young female real estate agent in 2008, I also examine the public's unceasing and often blatant curiosity about such happenings; this is what determines the need to know what actually happened.

Humankind's natural interest and demand to solve what appears to be unsolvable is what has kept these cases alive in the minds of dedicated investigators as well as historians and writers throughout the years.

Chapter One

The Murder of Constable Johnston Cochrane

~

On June 2, 1859, Constable Johnston Cochrane left Fort Victoria on foot to make an arrest. He was looking for a person suspected of shooting a pig. In those days, shooting livestock was a crime of the highest order.

Cochrane was last seen walking over the Craigflower Bridge at approximately 3:00 PM as he headed toward the area of Craigflower but, after a thorough search, he apparently could not find his suspect. Around 5:00 PM he was seen leaving that area in order to cross back over the Gorge Waterway and return to the fort. He never made it.

The next morning, his body was found in the brush a few feet off Craigflower Road. He had been shot twice, once in the upper lip and once in the temple. The second bullet had proved to be fatal.

Cochrane, an Irishman who had lived for many years in the United States before coming to Fort Victoria, was employed by the Colony of Vancouver Island as a police constable, and his main job was to keep the peace in and around the fort. It was not an easy line of work. Victoria was three years away from incorporation and was still nothing more than a rough, fun-loving and somewhat unruly western town.

Fort Victoria had been that way since the year earlier when thousands of transients and prospective miners arrived from all parts of the world in search of the elusive gold they assumed was abundant in the Cariboo area on the mainland. Fort Victoria was the stopping-off place for many of those gold-seekers, causing the peaceful solitude of the fort to change virtually overnight. A tent town had grown alongside the fort confines, and the mood and atmosphere of Victoria altered considerably. Suddenly, the village setting with a population of approximately 500 people turned into a rowdy area full of excited humanity all anxious to head to the gold fields and find their fortunes.

But Constable Cochrane was a man dedicated to his job and he enjoyed the excitement of all the changes going on around him. A mediator by nature, he was easily able to settle arguments, arrest drunks and mostly keep the peace. He felt his work was important because he believed that one day in the not too distant future, the fort would become a respectable and important city in the West.

Although policing might have been viewed as an unpopular occupation among those who liked to bend the law (and, back then, many did just that), Cochrane rarely complained about his job. Despite the numerous scuffles in which he became involved, he never imagined he had any real enemies.

However, on that particular June day, someone thought otherwise. Lurking in the bushes, an enemy had waited for the chance to kill him. And one enemy was all that was needed to end the life of a man who, to the best of his ability, had always upheld and honoured the law.

Two shots rang out, disturbing the comparative quietness of that day, and Cochrane became the first police officer in Victoria killed in the line of duty, apparently dying almost instantly. His body was later discovered on the side of the road by a man known as Francois Pressci, who immediately reported his gruesome find to the authorities. Before long, a full-scale investigation was underway into Cochrane's murder.

Despite the ongoing investigation, Cochrane's burial took place on June 4. Several suspects had already come under intense scrutiny by then, including Pressci, the man who had first discovered Cochrane's body. The issues and suspicions concerning Pressci were quickly dropped because no motive or any other contributing evidence could be found.

A second suspect was Joseph Lewis, better known in Victoria as "Portuguese Joe," who had come up against Cochrane on several occasions. On June 21, Portuguese Joe was arrested and charged with the crime but was released from custody 10 days later because of his so-called "watertight" alibi concerning his whereabouts at the time and place of the murder.

Meanwhile, the newspapers of the day continued to blame the local "Indian population" for the crime. The reasoning behind this line of thought was that Constable Cochrane had recently helped Sheriff Heaton remove several First Nations people from a Native settlement near the fort, an action that was not popular at the time. The First Nations people were annoyed that they had lost their homes and resented being treated this way. Was Cochrane's murder on that late afternoon in June simply retaliation for the actions of law enforcement officials?

Today, little is known about Johnston Cochrane's short but dedicated life to his police career. Records show he was a 36-year-old married man with children. A public fund was immediately set up for his family to help them in their time of need.

Cochrane's final resting place is in the "Old Burying Grounds," which today is known as Pioneer Square and is alongside the Anglican Cathedral at Quadra and Meares streets in Victoria. And in 1995, a memorial was erected in the square for all those who had died in the service of the Crown during the mid-1800s.

In 1996, however, when the Victoria Police Department moved its offices to a new state-of-the-art $18-million building on Caledonia Avenue, a memorial cairn was erected in the front of the new building for the five police officers, including Constable Cochrane, who had been killed in the line of duty since the police force was first incorporated in 1858.

The memorial cairn reads: "In memory of those officers who lost their lives serving the Crown and the citizens of Victoria." It then lists their names: 1859–Constable Johnston Cochrane; 1864–Constable John Curry; 1921–Constable Robert Forster; 1927–Constable Albert E. Wells; 1959–Constable Earle M. Doyle.

~

Cochrane's murder was never solved, and it became one of the first unsolved mysteries to plague Victoria throughout the coming years.

Chapter Two

Who Killed William Robinson?

~

Like many other African Americans, William Robinson immigrated to Salt Spring Island in British Columbia in the late 1850s to flee the United States' reprehensible practice of slavery leading up to the American Civil War.

Robinson was a middle-aged, peace-loving man from New Jersey, where he had left his wife and four children. He wanted to experience first-hand life in Canada before moving his family. Perhaps hoping for a better life in Canada, he took advantage of Governor James Douglas' offer to encourage black immigration to Salt Spring Island, one of the Gulf Islands off Vancouver Island.

For some years, Robinson farmed his land and lived alone in a somewhat isolated cabin on Salt Spring Island. He mostly kept to himself but did attend church regularly. He was planning to return to New Jersey to move his family sometime in 1868, but fate had other plans for him.

One evening in early March of that year, while eating his dinner alone in his cabin, he was shot in the back and died instantly. Police immediately launched an extensive investigation to uncover the motive for this gruesome and seemingly pointless killing. But it would be more than a year before the case was solved. Even then, critics wondered if there was more to Robinson's killing than the official account suggested. His murder was one of three that occurred on Salt Spring Island in the space of less than two years in which all the victims were black. Were all three killings racially motivated and were they all connected?

William Robinson's murder generated the most interest of the three because his case was the only one in which a suspect was eventually arrested, found guilty and hanged. Yet questions lingered about the suspect's guilt.

Initially, investigators thought there were three possible motives for Robinson's murder. The first was simply robbery, which would account for certain missing items in his cabin. The second, because of the murders of two other black men, was a hatred of black people. The third motive, deemed somewhat unlikely, was that Robinson had been killed for his land and the effects of his estate. This motive was the most far-fetched because a later probate of Robinson's estate revealed it was worth the paltry sum of $202.87, which included the value of his apparel, a purse, some bacon, a small quantity of oats, some cut hay, five small pigs and sundry improvements on his land worth $100. A probate fee of $89.66 for the cost of his coffin and burial as well as lawyer's fees, which included postage and travelling expenses to Victoria to file documents at court, was subtracted from the overall value. That left the value of Robinson's estate at $113.21, which hardly seems a strong enough motive to kill someone. His pre-empted acreage, however, was another matter that would soon come to light.

The murders of all three black men were initially blamed on a member of the First Nations band in the area. In William Robinson's case, a Native man from the Penelakut tribe known as Tshuanahusset (Tom) was arrested. An all-white jury found him guilty of murder, and Tom was sentenced to death. But was Tom really the killer? And why was he even arrested and convicted when there were three other possible suspects?

The first suspect was a man named Manuel Duett, a Salt Spring Island settler who farmed 150 acres in the Burgoyne Bay area. For reasons unknown, Salt Spring Island constable Henry Sampson named him as a possible suspect when Robinson's body was initially found.

A second suspect was the chief witness for the prosecution at Tom's trial, a man known as Sue Tas, or Dick. He was a 17-year-old First Nations man who could not read or write and had no particular trade. He was initially charged with accessory to murder as he admitted to being with Tom at the time Robinson was killed. Justice of the Peace John Morley arrested Dick on April 7, 1869, but Dick was discharged on

June 4 when the authorities could find no evidence that he had played a part in the actual crime.

The most unlikely suspects were the Bittancourt brothers (Estalon and Manuel). The Bittancourt family hailed from the Azores, a region of Portugal. After leaving the country, they had sailed to Australia to work in the gold fields. They arrived in Victoria, BC, in 1863, bought a sloop and transported fuel in the Gulf Islands for a living. The Bittancourts eventually moved to Salt Spring Island and became close friends with other Catholic families on the island.

Following Robinson's death, the Bittancourts had purchased his land and used the wharf site there to establish an even more successful transport business, amassing a fortune as a result. It could be argued the family had benefitted the most from Robinson's death but did that mean they were involved in his murder?

According to the newspapers of the day, Robinson was last seen at church on the Sunday evening before his death. An unnamed man who occasionally visited him reported he had some goods for Robinson that had just arrived on the island by boat. The man had made several visits to Robinson's cabin that day to deliver them but could not make contact with Robinson.

Finally, the man returned to the home the following Saturday and decided to remove some of the packing material between the logs of the cabin in order to peek inside as the cabin apparently had no windows. He saw a pair of boots on the floor and poked at one of them with a stick but got no response. He immediately sounded the alarm that something was terribly wrong.

Constable Henry Sampson did not arrive on the scene until Monday. He forced his way into the cabin and, to his horror, discovered Robinson on the floor lying on his back with a box, on which he had apparently been sitting, between his knees. Robinson was holding a knife in one hand; it appeared he had been eating supper when he was shot in the back and had most probably fallen backwards. By all accounts, he had been dead for approximately one week.

At Tom's trial in June 1869, Sampson described the gruesome scene to the court.

> *Early in the month of March 1868, I received informa-tion that William Robinson, who lived in a house on Salt Spring Island, near the steamboat landing, was murdered in his house. I went to the house and found the door locked. I forced one of the logs in, in which the house was built, and passed into the house. I saw Robinson lying on the floor on his back.*

> *The house was built of logs; it stood east and west, north and south. The door was in the north side and about in the center. There was a bed in the west end; there was no window in the house. The fireplace was in the east end*

and a plank, which served for a table, was fastened against the south side of the house, near the east end. I saw blood on the floor under the back of Robinson and there was congealed blood round his nose. His clothes were burst at the back. I did not move the body. The deceased held in his left hand a case knife. There was a plate and a cup and saucer on the table. There was some food on the plate, and it appeared as though he was eating when he was shot. I looked round the house and observed that a good many things were missing that I had frequently seen in the house. The articles that I missed were a gun, a chest, an axe, a coat of the deceased, and several other familiar articles.

I found on the floor a ball, which I now produce. I saw a mark on a log as if a ball had struck it and glanced. There were two holes in the body, one in the back, just below the shoulder blades, and the other in the breast, a little higher, as if the ball had passed through the body inclining upwards. The mark in the log in the side of the house was in range with the two holes in the body, if the man was sitting at the table when he was shot. From the appearance of the holes in the body, and the mark on the wall, I would judge that the man was shot from the fireplace whilst sitting at the table eating.

Many inaccuracies in Sampson's testimony would have been questioned in today's legal system, but it should be remembered it was 1869 and the legal system in the colony was still in its infancy.

If, for example, Robinson had been shot in the back as Sampson testified, it was more likely the murder victim would have fallen forward onto his makeshift table rather than backward to the floor. It also seems unlikely the constable could have assessed, at first glance, exactly what articles were missing from the cabin.

In addition, a piece of evidence from a crime, such as the "ball" Sampson described, would hardly have been kept in his possession until the trial. It would have been stored under police protection as "important evidence" in the case. The mere word of Sampson, a constable and farmer, would hold little weight in a court of law today because medical experts would be required to give details of how the ball had entered the body.

Sampson also stated that he had "received information that Robinson had been murdered in his house." How would anyone have known, prior to going inside the cabin, that a murder had taken place? After all, Robinson could have died from natural causes.

The constable also maintained that on other occasions when he had visited Robinson, he had always seen a "double-barrel shotgun hanging over the fireplace, and a large heavy axe nearby." A handsaw was also missing from the cabin, as was a coat Sampson stated he "searched all over the house for."

It was the sworn testimonies of John Norton, a farmer on Salt Spring Island, taken on April 2, and that of Dick on April 7, that led to Tom's arrest. Norton's testimony, sworn before a justice of the peace in the District of Cowichan, read:

About a week since, some strange Indians were fishing near my house; one of them told me he knew who it was that killed William Robinson of Salt Spring Island. He said that it was a Chemainus Indian named Tom that shot him and that an Indian [Dick] from Plumpers Pass [now Active Pass] was with him, and that the gun taken out of the Robinson's house was in a box at the Chemainus Ranch. I did not know the Indian that told me this, but I know the Indian from Plumpers Pass, and I believe I also know the murderer. The Indian told me that the Indian boy that was with Tom when he committed the murder would tell about it if he was asked.

Dick gave his version of events in his own sworn testimony on April 7, 1869.

About one year since, I was at Chemainus when an Indian named Tom said he would go home with me to Plumpers Pass. We went in a canoe together. We called at Salt Spring Island. Tom went up to Robinson's house. I stayed in the canoe till I got cold. I then went up to the house and warmed myself at the fire. When I got to the house Robinson was cooking some food. The Indian Tom was sitting near the fire; he had his gun with him. Tom said if he shot the black man I was to look for all the good things. I was afraid and went out of the house. Before I went out of the house Robinson had sat down to his food. After I got out of the house I heard a gun fired and Tom called me to come in. I went to the door and looked in and saw the black man lying on the floor. I saw blood running out of his nose, and from his back. Tom told me to come in and get some things but I said no.

Tom then took the gun down from the ceiling, he also took a saw, an auger, a box and a cart. Tom took them down into the canoe. After Tom had taken the things out of the house he locked the door and took the key out and threw the key into the salt water. Tom told me to take the box and cart. I would not take them. We then went back to Chemainus. I would not have any of the things. I saw Tom put the box on a shelf in his house. I also saw him with the gun belonging to Robinson in his own house. There was only Tom's wife in the house at Chemainus when we got back with the things.

I staid [sic] at Chemainus about five days after the potlatch and then went back to Plumpers Pass. I was afraid to tell sooner. Tom told me not to tell anybody. I only told my friends that Tom had killed the black man at Salt Spring Island.

This testimony, if believed, was damning and, despite the many loopholes in the case, such as unreliable witnesses and tampering of physical evidence, Tom was arrested that same day, one year after the murder. Tom made a statement upon his arrest that was both simple and straightforward: "I don't know what the witness Dick wants to say. Perhaps he wants to see me killed. I have been sick two years. I went to New Westminster and got 'fire sick' and could not go about. Mr. Franklin there knew me to be a good Indian and made me a constable."

Obviously trying to show that he was an honourable and upright person, and despite insisting he was innocent of the crime, Tom was arrested and moved to a jail in Victoria, where he awaited trial. Records indicated he was 26 years old, stood five-feet-five and had dark hair and a dark complexion. He had no trade and no "peculiar markings" and could neither read nor write.

The media of the day were obviously biased against First Nations people, and an editorial in April 1869 might have also contributed to Tom's arrest.

Salt Spring Island is among the first of our East Coast dependencies. A number of farms have been located by industrious men who have brought them into a very high state of cultivation.... A Tribe of Indians are located on the Island who, failing any other kind of excitement, murder a settler now and then by way of a change, and carry off his property to the bush, where it is secreted till the little puff of sensation is passed; the booty is then brought out and duly divided.

Such things have occurred three or four times, yet none of the murderers except "Dick" now in custody, have been brought to justice....

It is well known that the perpetrators of all the robberies and murders, except Dick are at large on the Island...

Several of the settlers have already left the Island and others are seriously thinking of doing so even at the sacrifice of all their property....

Judging from the description of the present state of feeling amongst the natives, as related to us by a gentleman just down from there, some measures must be taken without delay.

Tom's trial, under the jurisdiction of Chief Justice Needham, began on June 2, 1869, with the Attorney General acting for the Crown and a Mr. D. Babbington Ring for the accused.

Needham was chief justice of Vancouver Island and eventually of New Caledonia (to later become British Columbia) from 1865 until 1870. It was said he refused to allow barristers to appear in his court without wearing white shirts, wigs and gowns while he always appeared with full wig and scarlet robes trimmed with fur. In 1870 he was appointed Chief Justice of

Trinidad and was later knighted. He retired to England, where he died in 1895 at age 83.

Babbington Ring was a 65-year-old lawyer from Scotland who had arrived in Victoria in 1859. He was thought to be something of an eccentric in early colonial society and had often physically threatened Attorney General George Carey; on one occasion, one of Carey's supporters challenged Ring to a duel.

Ring had defended many other Native people before acting on Tom's behalf and was known to be a sympathetic member of the Legislative Assembly in matters concerning First Nations people.

On June 3, the day after Tom's trial began, *The British Colonist* included an article with the headline "Threats" and stated, "We learn that the Indian [Dick] who gave evidence against the Indian convicted of the murder of Robinson, has been threatened with death if he returns home. He has been outlawed by his chief."

The trial, however, continued, with many witnesses being called, both for the prosecution and for the defence. Two Chinook interpreters, Jonathan Martin and Robert McMillan, were also present during the proceedings to help when needed. The accused, described simply as "Tom, Indian Murderer," pled not guilty.

During the examinations and cross-examinations in the coming days, much was made of the axe found in Tom's possession. It was believed to have been one of the items the killer took from Robinson's cabin. It was distinctive in appearance and could not, according to many of the witnesses for the prosecution, have been confused with any other axe.

One witness in particular, John Norton, stated he recognized the axe because of the pieces cut off at the end and also a little knot in the wood. He said Robinson made his own axe handles that were individualistic in style.

Tom's brother Charlie, who was a witness for the defence, told the court he had made the axe handle allegedly found in Tom's house, stating it definitely wasn't William Robinson's axe.

Another witness for the defence, Thomas George Askew, a sawmill owner and a prominent white settler at Chemainus, claimed he had sold an unusual axe head to Tom, which again cast doubt as to whether or not it had been Robinson's axe.

However, Armstead Buckner, who testified for the Crown, gave damning testimony concerning the axe in question, which supported Tom's guilt. He stated it was a left-handed axe, that Robinson was left-handed and that he definitely recognized the handle as being the one on Robinson's axe.

On cross examination when recalled to the stand, Henry Sampson stated he went to Robinson's house in the company of one "Clark Whims, a coloured boy, and they stopped there until the evening." Many other settlers were also present at the murder scene, which gives rise to the possibility someone had tampered with the evidence. The coroner, Mr. John Morley, did not arrive at the scene right away, but when he did, his examination of the body lasted almost four hours.

Sampson also reiterated that two other men were initially accused by Mr. Morley of being murder suspects—Manuel Duett and Clark Whims. In fact, Sampson stated, "everyone was suspected. Harrison, another coloured man, was examined. All were examined, ladies and all."

Nonetheless, it had taken a year before anyone had been arrested, and even then many people still doubted whether Tom was guilty.

On June 23, 1869, 23 men had been sworn in as a grand jury for an unrelated larceny case. What is particularly interesting about the jury members is that apparently 12 of them also sat on the jury at Tom's trial. It was not disclosed, however, as to which 12 were the jurists, but the entire list of names reads like a "who's who" of early Victoria:

R. Burnaby (foreman of the jury)
Thomas Lett Stahlschimdt (a respected Victoria merchant
    engaged in the mercantile business)

Richard Carr (father of artist Emily Carr, born in 1871)

George Isaac Stuart

John Wilkie (upper-class resident of Victoria and a leading merchant in the city)

D. Leneven

M.T. Johnson

Thomas Lowe

Thomas Hickman Tye (owner and operator of Hickman Tye Hardware Company in Victoria)

A.J. Langley

George Robinson Fardon (famous photographer in early Victoria)

M. Moore

Benjamin Pitt Griffin (adventurer and owner of The Boomerang Inn in Victoria)

Roderick Finlayson (Hudson's Bay Company employee who became superintendent of Fort Victoria until 1849 and later laid out the plan for the city of Victoria)

Rout Harvey (arrived in Victoria in 1861 from Bury St. Edmunds, England, and worked in the wholesale business)

Edward Mallandaine (publisher of *Victoria's First Directory* who was married to Louisa Townsend, a passenger aboard the famous 1862 bride ship the *Tynemouth)*

T. Allsop

H.B. Good

T. Nuttall

R. Beaven

W.C. Ward

Lumley Franklin (second mayor of Victoria, in 1865)

G. Gillon

At precisely 4:55 PM on June 24, the jury in the case of "Tom The Indian versus the Crown" was dismissed to deliberate on the evidence and reach a verdict. They returned a mere 10 minutes later, and foreman R. Burnaby read the verdict of "guilty" to the court. Judge Needham then sentenced the prisoner to "death by hanging."

Justice was swift in those days. One month later, on July 24, the *British Colonist* wrote, "The execution of the Chemainus Indian will take place at 7:00 this morning. The scaffold was erected last evening in the lot adjoining the barracks. The prisoner was visited by his wife and mother yesterday and exhibited great concern."

Following his execution, Tom's body was delivered to his friends for burial on the nearby reserve. Throughout the rest of the day, "a great wailing" could be heard from the family and friends of the deceased.

The evidence against Tom had seemed both overwhelming and conclusive according to the laws of the day, but the case contained so many holes that in the decades since Tom's trial, historians have continued to challenge the verdict.

One last substantive detail contributing to the doubt was that yet another black man was murdered after Tom's execution, giving rise to the possibility that Robinson's murderer was still at large—if this had indeed been a racial crime.

In addition, Sylvia Stark, a member of another black family on Salt Spring Island, believed that a man named Willie Selcalcher, a First Nations person who transported goods and groceries for Salt Spring settlers, was responsible for the death of several blacks and whites during those early years. Selcalcher was charged with the murder of one Giles Curtis nearly a decade after Robinson's murder but was acquitted. Could Selcalcher have been the "unnamed man" who stated he had received no response at Robinson's cabin when he tried to make a delivery there in March 1868?

These possibilities were never fully pursued the year before Tom was arrested and charged with the Robinson's murder. It perhaps seemed easier to condemn a First Nations person in light of public opinion against Native people at that time.

One last suspicious fact concerns John Norton, a witness for the prosecution. It seemed strange that Norton had frequently involved himself in the so-called "Indian outrages" on the island and was often "first on the scene" at these events. Born in 1823, he was said to be of Portuguese origin and had arrived on Vancouver Island in 1859, taking up farmland on Salt Spring Island in 1861. He was married to a young woman of mixed race, with whom he raised 13 children.

It was Norton who had first alerted the authorities to a crime at Robinson's cabin and also gave them information about Native people threatening other settlers. In addition, he was the person who produced pieces of incriminating evidence against Tom, including an auger from the cabin that he later conveniently lost.

By 1891, Norton's land on Salt Spring Island was among the most valuable, worth $10 per acre—more than twice the island average. And even more suspect was his connection and friendship with the Bittancourt brothers (also from Portugal), who also became wealthy after they acquired Robinson's land following his death. Was there a connection?

There are so many variables in the William Robinson murder case that it makes for a true mystery. The inconsistencies in the case were noted and pondered upon by one particular observer at the trial, a man known as William Smithe, but better known later as Amor de Cosmos, who in 1883 became premier of BC.

In June 1869, Smithe attended Tom's trial in Victoria while waiting for a steamer heading for San Francisco. For many years he was a noted journalist and correspondent, with strong and colourful views on most topics. It was inevitable that he would eventually run for politics. An opinionated man, Smithe was just one of a legion of individuals who raised doubts about Tom's guilt and the assembled evidence against him.

It is perhaps appropriate that the last word on Robinson's murder should go to Sylvia Stark, whose *Reminiscences* appears on the Great Unsolved Mysteries in Canadian History website.

> *Mr. Robinson, a very devoted Sunday school teacher, often sang this old sweet song to his pupils; "Children of the Heavenly King, as we Journey Let Us Sing." It was sung in the old way with all the quavers of a spiritual. I have often heard my mother sing it just as they sang it in the old log cabin school house where she first learned it.*

> *One Sunday he sang to those brave children of the brave pioneers for the last time. He told me that the next Sunday would be his farewell meeting. He had written to his wife asking her to come west, but she refused to come to a wild country where the Indians were hostile so now he was going back to her.*

> *When the next Sunday came and he failed to arrive at Church, the congregation waited with growing uneasiness. Then a party went to his house at Vesuvius Bay where they found him slain in his cabin where he had lived alone.*

Once again, Stark's comments reveal the conflicting statements in the timeline of how and when Robinson was first found and by whom. Each person's story varies in some way or is coloured in one aspect or another.

It seems particularly odd that with such a small population on Salt Spring Island at that time (approximately 70 people when Robinson was killed, and a mere 90 by 1871), the right murderer could not have been apprehended sooner.

Was this a crime of racial prejudice against the black population on the island? Or could Robinson's wife have been right about her fear of "hostile Indians" who were supposedly killing and stealing from all the settlers at will?

Or, most ominous of all, could this crime have involved land acquisitions far more devious and manipulative than anyone at that time could ever have imagined?

Today, 143 years later, the answers are still unknown.

Chapter Three

The Cariboo Mile 108 Hotel Murders

~

Back in the 19th century, many mysteries and unsolved crimes were connected to the old Cariboo Trail. By far the most gruesome were the events that supposedly happened at the Mile 108 Hotel in the Cariboo area of north-central British Columbia. The hotel at that time was owned and operated by Scottish-born Agnes (sometimes spelled "Agnus") McVee during the 1870s.

The gold rushes of 1858 and 1862 were a distant memory. A decade later, the notorious but captivating McVee was dealing in another type of "gold"—lodging, the sale of food and liquor and, more specifically, young women, many of whom came through the Cariboo area fleeing miserable situations in other parts of BC. Most were hoping to find a rich husband in the Cariboo.

In March 1875, a well-to-do miner named Henry Dawson arrived at the infamous hotel looking for such a young woman. He had heard of Agnes McVee's own incredible beauty and of her reputation for supplying "the best girl at a bargain price." He was in particular need of a long-term relationship with a woman who could cook for him and take care of all his needs at his mine in the neighbouring area. He was prepared to pay the required amount, little knowing the terrible price he would actually end up paying.

Dawson had at least $11,000 worth of gold on his person, some in the form of dust and the rest in nuggets, and he was more than ready to spend some of it on the best woman he could find. He was a lonely man and was also somewhat gullible. As he rode up to the three-storey hotel at Mile 108, a man came out to greet him, introducing himself as Jim, McVee's so-called husband. He offered to tend to Dawson's horse and told him to go inside, buy himself a drink and a meal and rest from his travels.

Inside, Dawson met with Al Riley, the bartender. Dawson told him the nature of his business and, in return, Al volunteered the information that he was McVee's son-in-law. He also told Dawson that only his mother-in-law decided the price set on a girl and that she was currently away, having recently gone to Fort Kamloops on business. She was, however, expected to return later that night.

Meanwhile, Dawson was offered a hearty meal and the best in whiskey. In fact, he was plied with one glass after another until he was feeling particularly drowsy and content as he settled in front of the roaring fire. Al then went outside where

Agnes McVee was actually lurking in the dark, watching the entire proceedings, which had all been planned ahead of time. She then handed Al a rifle and told him what to do.

Like Jim, the man who had tended to Dawson's horse and did most of the errands around the hotel, Al was terrified of the dictatorial Agnes, a powerful woman both in personality and physique. Neither of the men dared to cross her or question her demands. So Al rested the rifle on the open window ledge and took steady aim at Henry Dawson's back. The shot roared through the silent night and easily met its mark, blowing a large hole in Dawson's back that killed him instantly.

Agnes and Al then went inside and made sure Dawson was really dead. Then, lifting the corpse between them, they took it outside to the wagon where Jim was waiting to drive it to the nearby lake and drop it into the water.

Some weeks later, when the body was eventually discovered, the local authorities reported that the late Henry Dawson "was most foully murdered by a robber who made off with his personal possessions and his horse." With robbery being a frequent occurrence in the Cariboo, no further investigation was carried out.

Dawson's murder was one of many such incidents in the coming years, and Agnes McVee, Al and Jim were allegedly responsible for most of them.

Rumour has it that many young women, merchants, miners and other prospective buyers all visited the Mile 108 Hotel during those years and most, if not all, met their demise in a similar fashion. Agnes stole from the rich ones and buried some of the stolen money in or around the hotel. Her stash included gold coins and nuggets or actual cash. Meanwhile, Jim would steal the victims' horses, and whenever he had collected several of them, he took the horses to Fort Kamloops, where he was believed to be a wealthy horse dealer.

Many young runaway women were kept in Agnes' basement, and a few were sold to rich men. Those who couldn't be sold were killed.

Agnes' ill-begotten gains were said to amount to about $150,000, and she was fast becoming an extremely rich woman. She ran an almost-perfect criminal scam and, having little or no conscience or decency in her soul, continued on her evil path with the assistance of the two men who did her bidding.

All was going well until the early 1880s when something completely unexpected happened to Agnes. A tall, handsome gambler from Fort Langley named MacDonald arrived at the hotel, and Agnes fell instantly in love with him. He, like many before him, had come to the area in search of a young female companion.

Both Al and Jim assumed MacDonald would meet the same fate as the many who came before him, but this time Agnes decided to change her plans. She did not give Al the rifle but instead told him they would sell the handsome stranger a girl. Agnes went into the hotel and, turning on all her charm, flirted outrageously with MacDonald, offering to sell him a beautiful 17-year-old girl for the price of $4000, if, in turn, he promised to return to her in a month's time. Agnes produced the girl from the basement and the deal was made. MacDonald left the hotel for the stable to saddle up his horses, tying the girl onto one of them. He then rode away into the night. Agnes, still besotted with MacDonald and already thinking about his return, barely noticed that Jim had left the hotel in a jealous rage. Much later, Al ran to her with the news that Jim had just returned and that he had noticed Jim had a pistol in his belt and that he had hid a sack in the hayloft.

Agnes screamed for her husband to come to her immediately. He reluctantly admitted he had followed MacDonald and the girl and had killed MacDonald. Jim gave Agnes the sack of gold coins worth at least $8000, saying, "Now we have $12,000 for our trouble instead of just the $4000 for the girl."

But Agnes was incensed. How dare he take over and decide what should be done! Only she could do that as she ran the operation. However, Agnes kept her anger in check, and the following morning she even appeared to be in a forgiving mood.

She cooked Jim and Al a wholesome breakfast and did not refer to the escapade of the night before other than to say to Jim, "It's over and done with. After all, we have his money and there is no cause for us to quarrel."

But Agnes was a vindictive woman and did not forgive disobedience easily. In the middle of eating his breakfast, Jim suddenly complained of a violent pain and fell to the floor reeling in agony. Within minutes he was dead.

Al was astounded. He screamed at Agnes, "You've killed him! You must have put poison in his food!"

Agnes' smile was evil as she warned Al that if he spoke of what she had done, the same thing would happen to him. She then ordered him to dispose of the body in the usual way.

However, both Agnes and Al had overlooked one important fact—they had no way of knowing that while Jim had killed and robbed MacDonald, the young girl who had been with him was able to escape. Some police officers later found her wandering along the road. The girl told them McVee had kept her prisoner in the basement at the Mile 108 Hotel and that other young women were still there. She also said she had been sold to MacDonald and that he had been shot to death by a man named Jim. She described Jim as being the man who had brought food to her and the other girls each day while they were imprisoned at the hotel.

Meanwhile, just as Agnes and Al were preparing to carry Jim's body to the wagon at the back of the hotel, the law arrived on the scene. Agnes immediately had a cover story ready. She said her husband had accidentally eaten some rat poison and died immediately. She and Al were preparing his body for burial, she said, while weeping and bringing all her acting abilities to bear. Agnes denied all the other charges, saying she had never heard of a man named MacDonald nor had she sold him a young girl, and there were certainly no other girls at her establishment.

However, the police officers decided to search the property to make sure, and at that precise moment, Al lost his nerve and confessed everything, stating that his mother-in-law was the instigator of all the murders that had occurred in the Cariboo as well as the abductions of the girls. He told them where the girls were kept, and when the house was searched, eight young women, all chained together and near starvation, were found in the basement. Further investigation also revealed human bones in the ashes in the fireplace. It was later proved that Agnes McVee had burned to death some of the captive girls who were of no use to her.

Agnes McVee and Al Riley were immediately taken to nearby Fort Kamloops and then to New Westminster where they were both jailed and charged with kidnapping and murder. Unfortunately, when Agnes was arrested, she was never thoroughly searched and she had apparently kept some of the rat poison on her person. In June 1885, prior to standing trial, she ate the poison and died immediately. Al Riley had a separate trial, was found guilty of all charges and was subsequently hanged.

The gruesome slayings had finally ended, but the mystery concerning the money accumulated by Agnes McVee and her evil cohorts remained. In 1892, the Mile 108 Hotel was torn down and moved to the opposite side of the road, where the lumber was used to build a telegraph store and post office. The building still stands today as a historical site.

Most of the McVee story has been described in the area as simply a rumour blown out of proportion. The rumour was said to have originated from "an old-timer" and was later described in a booklet entitled *Lost Treasure in BC* (now out of print) by Larry Lazeo of Fort Langley. Unfortunately, strong historical documentation for the story has never been found despite searches in numerous archives, including Kamloops, New Westminster and Victoria. No actual documents of ownership showing McVee ran the 108 Mile Hotel in that decade were ever discovered. There were also no missing person's reports during that time period or police records of the actual arrests or Al's trial to substantiate the story. Even more curious, no death certificates were issued for either Agnes McVee or Al Riley.

One solid piece of evidence does exist that lends some credence to this tale. In 1929, a farmer in the area unearthed $2500 in gold nuggets and coins, presumed to be some of Agnes McVee's ill-begotten gains. A similar amount, this time of $6000, was found when Block Brothers Realty built an airstrip in the area a few years later.

In 2006, Red Barn Productions filmed a story of the grisly events for CTV's *Travel and Discovery* series. The Agnes McVee story can also be found on a BC government historical information web page. However, even that article is subtitled, "A rumor has it."

The entire McVee fortune, believed to be valued between $100,000 and $150,000, has never been located. Does the money still lie buried somewhere along the old Cariboo Trail or is the story mostly myth and fantasy? You decide.

Chapter Four

Who Was the Real
Ten Mile Point Murderer?

~

E arly in November 1898, the *Victoria Times-Colonist* newspaper reported on a murder that shocked the area of Ten Mile Point in BC's capital city. The article stated that a young man had been brutally slain as he slept in his wilderness cabin that overlooked the Haro Strait east of Victoria. The man's body had apparently been there for approximately 12 days before it was discovered. Even worse was that the young man's cabin mate, an old family friend named Billy Hammond, had completely disappeared and was suspected of the deadly deed.

The killing was graphically described as one of the most horrific homicides the province had ever seen, and the newspaper stated that although there were no apparent witnesses to the crime, the interior of the cabin "screamed murder!"

The *Times-Colonist* continued:

A little cluster of bed clothes which lay in a heap on the floor showed plainly that they were hurriedly torn away by the murderer just before he swung the axe which sent

a promising young man to eternity and earned the mur-
derer the everlasting fear of the hangman's noose....

The victim was identified as 26-year-old Henry Smith.
The cabin in which his mutilated body had been found was
owned by his father but rented to their friend, Billy Hammond.
Young Henry had often enjoyed hiking out toward Ten Mile
Point for woodcutting or hunting trips and to visit Billy but,
on this particular occasion, Henry had been gone for longer
than usual and his father had become concerned. The senior
Smith had hiked to the cabin with his friend George Deans to
see if Henry was all right.

Upon arriving at the cabin, the two men immediately
became suspicious because everything was so quiet and the
cabin door was padlocked. Peering through the murky window,
they noticed Henry's clothes were still hanging on the wall.
Henry's father was sure that something must be wrong, so he
and George broke down the door and went inside. The sight that
met their eyes was horrendous.

A pile of blood-soaked bedclothes lay in the middle of
the room with a blood-stained axe nearby. Henry's lifeless body
was found stuffed in a box beneath the bed.

The report in the *Times-Colonist* explicitly described the
gruesome scene: "...the murderer had obviously sprung upon
him [Henry Smith] as he slept, and the axe with its gory coating
was thrown aside...with a seeming desire to hide the evidence of
the crime. The murderer then dragged the body from the bed

and attempted to stuff it as tightly as possible into the 'sleeping box' under the bed."

Although the police could not prove Billy Hammond was the killer, Henry's father felt convinced that Hammond had killed his son. He knew that Hammond held an old grudge against him concerning a long-overdue debt and, despite Hammond's friendship with the victim, Smith firmly believed that Hammond had committed this atrocity as payback.

The police were not so easily persuaded of Hammond's guilt, despite his mysterious disappearance. They knew he had always been devoted to young Henry Smith and had paid more attention to the boy than did his own father. It seemed impossible to believe that Hammond would have slaughtered Henry simply out of revenge.

Although Hammond was small in stature (five-foot-three), he had once served as a bartender and bouncer at the King's Head Hotel on Johnson Street in town so he must have been physically strong. He could quite possibly have attacked Henry. But it was also widely known that Hammond was devoted to Henry Smith, so there was no apparent motive to commit such a crime—only the word of Henry's father. And why would Hammond suddenly decide to kill the young man he cared so much about? Although obviously a crime of passion, it had not been committed in a fit of anger during an argument because the victim had seemingly been asleep in bed when he was attacked.

Billy Hammond's past provided no other clues for the police to follow up on. Thirty years earlier, both he and Henry Smith Sr. had arrived in Esquimalt to the west of Victoria aboard the HMS *Sparrowhawk*. Hammond went on to work on various coastal steamers running between San Francisco and Alaska. After leaving the sea life behind, Hammond purchased 62 acres of land at Ten Mile Point from a man named William Deans and settled down as a farmer. A restless man by nature, Hammond soon grew bored and left for Omineca and the mine fields to try his luck there.

Once in a while, Hammond would return to Victoria, renewing his friendship with the Smiths and forming a bond with young Henry as the boy grew up. On one occasion, a report reached Victoria that Hammond had died, but this proved to be false. In the summer of 1891, he turned up yet again, this time looking somewhat emaciated and unkempt.

Around this time he relinquished his deed to his Ten Mile Point property and Smith Sr. took over the ownership of the land and cabin and even advanced Hammond some money, allowing him to live at the cabin on a rental basis. It was during this period that Henry Jr. enjoyed hiking out to the cabin to visit Hammond, and their friendship grew even more.

But Henry Smith Sr. believed Hammond might have held a grudge against him over the ownership of the cabin and had decided to take out his anger on Henry Jr. Could this have been the case? But why, if what Smith Sr. said was true, would Hammond hold a grudge when Smith had loaned him money and allowed him to live in the cabin?

The murder investigation continued for months and then took a rather surprising turn. Quite unexpectedly, another body was discovered near the railway tracks in Esquimalt on the outskirts of Victoria. Upon identification, the body proved to be that of Billy Hammond himself. Foul play was not suspected; it was believed Hammond had died of a heart attack.

And then came another startling revelation. Someone had been allowed to view Hammond's body and had identified him as being the same person who was seen running from the scene of a previous murder in Ashcroft, BC. And the date of that sighting coincided with one of Hammond's mysterious disappearances from Victoria some years earlier. The victim of that particular crime had been attacked and killed with a shovel—a *modus operandi* similar to Henry's murder in October 1898.

It was assumed that Billy Hammond, although small, was quite capable of attacking young Henry Smith on the night in question because many believed he had the strength of two men—and a temper to go along with it. But the mystery remained as to why he would have suddenly killed the son of an old friend, a boy he had grown to love like his own? What could his motive possibly have been? It made no sense.

The coroner's report had concluded that Henry Smith Jr. had died from wounds inflicted with an axe at the hands of

some person or persons unknown. The case remained closed
and eventually went cold over time. If Billy Hammond killed
Henry, it was a secret he took with him to the grave.

Despite innuendo and speculation, no one has ever
unravelled the truth of what really happened on that fateful
night over a century ago, leaving only the gossips and the historians to hypothesize and wonder.

Chapter Five

The Vicious Slaying of Agnes Bings

~

German-born Agnes Bings was a hardworking woman. She had to be, because in 1899 she was the sole supporter of her family in Victoria.

Her husband John had suffered a stroke a few years earlier and, although he had made a fairly good recovery, he was still unable to work. Instead, he stayed home and took care of their eight-year-old son Arthur while Agnes worked at her brother's bakery on Store Street, a 30-minute walk from her home in Victoria West.

According to Agnes' brother, William Jordan, on the evening of September 29, 1899, Agnes left the shop between 7:00 PM and 8:00 PM. She asked her brother to help her carry some parcels home, but he had to decline because he still had work to finish at the bakery before closing up for the night. Agnes was in a hurry to get home and make dinner for her husband and son, so she decided to leave her parcels at the shop.

It was dark and raining heavily when she left the shop. A strong wind was also blowing; in fact, it was a thoroughly miserable night. The walk between the shop and her home on Russell Street was not a pleasant one for a woman walking alone, even during good weather, but Agnes had done it many times before and was used to it. She set off at her usual steady pace.

She always took the shortest possible route, which meant crossing over the Esquimalt and Nanaimo (E & N) railway bridge. She would then traverse the railway trestle alongside today's Esquimalt Road and turn right to cross the First Nations Songhees reserve land as she headed toward Victoria West.

When Agnes did not return home by 8:00 PM, her husband began to worry. Pacing back and forth and opening and closing the front door to see if Agnes was coming, John fretted as the windstorm increased in intensity and there was still no sign of his wife. By 9:00 PM he became frantic, but he couldn't go out and search for his wife because he could not leave their sleeping son alone. The Bings did not own a telephone so he also couldn't contact his wife's brother at the shop or anyone else in town.

As the hours ticked by, he assumed and hoped that Agnes had decided to stay in town overnight because of the storm. By midnight he fell into a sporadic sleep.

At first light the next morning, John left the house to contact Agnes' brother and some friends in town to see if his wife had stayed overnight. But no one had seen her since she had left the bakery the evening before.

John became frantic as he headed to the police station, where Constable Robert Walker was immediately sent out to retrace the missing woman's steps. With John's description, the constable walked the same path that Agnes always took. At approximately 9:00 AM, as he turned right after crossing the E & N trestle, he noticed something lying in a hollow. On closer inspection, Walker discovered the nude and mutilated body of Agnes Bings.

Horror stricken by the condition of the woman's corpse, Constable Walker reported his gruesome find to his superiors. A manhunt began immediately. The *Colonist* reported the murder the following day:

> *On Friday evening, sometime between 7 and 8 o'clock, a woman was cruelly murdered on a well-travelled thoroughfare and within a few yards of occupied houses, and not until 12 hours later was her body found, so that the murderer had lots of time to cover up his tracks and get well away from the scene of his crime.*

This was by far the most atrocious murder that Victoria had ever seen at that time. Agnes Bings, a hardworking, respectable, 45-year-old wife and mother, had been brutally raped and murdered. The newspaper refused to publish more details of the crime, stating that they were "too revolting for publication."

The condition of the murdered woman's body confirmed she had fought desperately for her life. Her assailant must have had "super-human strength" according to the examining physician, Dr. R.L. Fraser. He suspected the killer had used a rope or strap to strangle her after he had performed unspeakable acts of rape and mutilation.

Initially, the murder was thought to be a robbery that had gone terribly wrong because two of Agnes' rings were missing from her fingers. It was assumed she had put up a fight when her attacker tried to steal the rings and this had provoked the robber into murdering her. Her purse was discovered some distance from her body, but it was empty, which again substantiated the theory of an attempted robbery.

Agnes' brother and John, however, maintained she would not have had much cash, if any, inside her purse. The most it could have contained was a few dollars, which could have infuriated the robber enough to kill her.

The location of the crime was another issue that came into play. Agnes' body was found near a First Nations reserve, so it was thought that a Native person could have committed the crime. However, this theory was quickly discounted because the newspapers stated that, "Indians seldom or never commit murder without provocation, and...do not mutilate a body the way Mrs. Bings' was."

It was soon agreed that a deranged person must have committed the murder. With this in mind, the police brought in for questioning anyone in town who had previously displayed abnormal behaviour. This included vagrants, those with criminal records or derelicts with deviant lifestyles. All of these individuals had to account for their whereabouts at the time of Agnes' murder. Rounding up these people also put the police in a good light—it made it appear they were working to protect the public from another such crime.

Unfortunately, the foul weather on the night of the murder thwarted the police investigation. The heavy rains that night washed away a good deal of what could have been helpful evidence, such as footprints or bloodstains.

The residents of Victoria were in a state of turmoil. Many people gathered outside the police station when it was announced that a suspect had been arrested. Everyone was hoping for a decisive end to the nightmare of possibly having a mad man on the loose.

It was learned that a man named Charles St. John had been apprehended a few yards from where Bings' purse had been located. He was seen to act in a strange manner and was brought in for intensive questioning. He told the police he had recently quit his job as a woodcutter on a Colwood farm and had hiked into town. By the time he reached the E & N trestle, he was in a delusional state, having existed on nothing but bread and water for days, which, he told the police, was his cure for leg cramps. He said he would be living at his father's View Street cottage or camping in Beacon Hill Park and insisted that he knew absolutely nothing about the crime.

After St. John underwent a medical examination and his story was thoroughly checked, he was released. The police's intense interrogation had convinced them he could not have been responsible for Bings' murder.

A few days before Agnes was killed, the nude body of a Native woman had been discovered in the same location where Agnes' body was found. Although her death had been attributed to natural causes, it resurrected the possibility that a First Nations person was responsible for Agnes Bings' murder.

Perhaps Agnes Bings' death on First Nations reserve land had been no coincidence, but the police had no indisputable evidence that suggested a Native person had committed the crime. In addition, there was no trace of the victim's clothing or her jewellery. In view of racial prejudice at that time, some people believed this proved a Native person had committed the crime. A Native person, they thought, might have been tempted to steal clothing or jewellery. Others, however, believed that a Native would not have stolen jewellery or committed such a violent act against a woman. A rumour even began circulating that the killer had returned to town the following day wearing Agnes Bings' clothing—a bizarre and monstrous thought.

The police then began searching the nearby harbour waters for Agnes' clothing, but found nothing. All clues were faithfully followed up, including the questioning by two officers at Esquimalt's Halfway House pub of a highly inebriated man who claimed to have information about the case. Again police drew a blank. Dissension between the Victoria Police Force and the Songhees Reserve population was also hindering the investigation.

A coroner's inquest held on October 2 brought new information to light. William Jordan, Agnes' brother, stated that he knew Agnes did not have more than a few cents in her purse on the night of her murder, and he also said she left her parcels behind, a fact the police did not appear to know before the inquest. Had Agnes been carrying the parcels with her, they likely would have been stolen.

The mystery of Agnes Bings' macabre killing continued, and Victoria residents were outraged that a well-liked, kindly woman had met such a disturbing end in their quiet, respectable city. Newspapers of the day reported that the killer must have had great strength because, although Agnes Bings was slight of build, everyone who knew her said she was a strong woman and most likely would have been able to fight off a less powerful attacker. This fact alone put fear into everyone who now pictured a demon of extraordinary strength still roaming free.

And that was when another far-fetched, bizarre aspect of Victorian life entered the mix. A Dr. Dumain and his "assistant" Miss Agnes Harris staged a séance at the scene of the murder in an attempt to recreate the crime. Miss Harris, in a reputed trance, began to recount the crime in detail.

She described the clothing of Agnes Bings and gave a vivid portrayal of a man coming up the railway tracks behind Agnes. Harris then stated the man committed the unspeakable crime, after which he wiped his bloodstained hands on the dead woman's stockings. She added that he had dropped the stockings into the water at the end of the trestle bridge and hurriedly left for the harbour in an attempt to catch a steamer and leave town, but no steamer was available at the time, so presumably he was still in the area. Her gory story then came to an abrupt end as Dr. Dumain gradually brought her out of her hypnotic state.

These macabre theatrics were performed two more times, each in front of a curious crowd. However, a reporter watching the events noted the performance was not a genuine séance but rather an attempt by Dr. Dumain to put Miss Harris under hypnosis and then will her to say what he was thinking. And this posed the question as to how Dr. Dumain knew so much about what had happened on the night of the murder and the description of the murderer. In the reporter's opinion, this knowledge made the good doctor highly suspect.

In addition, it was learned that Dr. Dumain had a benefactress, a certain Madame Hellier, who presumably supported him. Not long before Bings' murder, Madame Hellier's daughter had drowned in strange circumstances. Having this event recalled and brought to the public's attention encouraged Dr. Dumain to quickly conclude his séances and leave town.

For some unknown reason, the police did not investigate him further.

The provincial government then offered a reward of $750 for information leading to the arrest of Agnes' murderer, but this did not bring forth any additional information and, as time passed, the tragic crime seemed to have been forgotten. Even the diligent work of Police Chief Sheppard and his men that continued for several weeks didn't generate any new leads. However, all residents of the Songhees Reserve had accounted for their movements on the night in question, which positively eliminated them from involvement in the crime.

So who did Agnes Bings run into by the railway line on the night of September 29, 1899? History tells us that we might never know, but according to one writer in 1989, the tragedy could well have been avoided. He stated:

> The night before, a young dressmaker [Annie Duncan] had been accosted by a "rough looking" man while following the same route that would have been taken by Mrs. Bings. When the stranger had appeared beside her and asked if she were not afraid of the dark, the dressmaker had bravely ordered him away. At that precise moment two shipyard workers appeared and her unwanted companion had slipped away into the night.

> The feisty Miss Duncan reported her encounter to the police and Constable Walker—the very officer who would find Mrs. Bings' body—volunteered to accompany the

seamstress to her home the following night. But Miss
Duncan's nerve finally failed her and on that Friday
night she chose to remain in town with friends.

If Annie Duncan had accepted Constable Walker's offer
of an escort, they would have crossed Songhees Reserve at the
same time as Agnes Bings. Or if poor Agnes Bings had been
seen by shipyard workers on the night she was accosted, her
murderer might have slipped away into the night as he had when
he had met Duncan.

As with all murder cases, those closest to the victim are
always the first suspected of having committed the crime.
Both Agnes' husband and brother were thoroughly interro-
gated by the police but cleared of any involvement. It's likely
Agnes' brother felt considerable guilt for a long time afterward
for not insisting that he accompany his sister home on that
fateful night.

The Agnes Bings murder case remains unsolved.

Chapter Six
The Scottish Nightingale

~

On July 26, 1924, an upscale house in Shaughnessy Heights near Point Grey, Vancouver, was the scene of a police investigation of monumental proportions. It was an investigation that took many strange twists and turns over a long period of time but was never successfully solved.

The house at 3851 Osler Avenue was owned by Richard Baker and his wife, Blanche, the daughter of the wealthy and influential Alexander Duncan McRae. McRae lived at nearby Hycroft Manor. At the time of the police investigation, Richard's brother, Frank L. Baker, a prominent exporter of pharmaceutical drugs, was living in the Osler Avenue house. Frank's own home on Nelson Avenue was being renovated and Richard had offered Frank and his family the home while they were away.

The police were called to the home on that hot Sunday in July to investigate the death of Scottish nursemaid Janet Smith, an attractive 22-year-old who worked for the Frank Baker family. The year earlier, Frank's wife Doreen had hired

Janet in London, England, to look after the couple's young daughter Rosemary for a salary of $20 per month. Janet was born in Perth, Scotland, and had grown up in a working-class area of London before the Bakers had hired her. After the family and Janet spent a short time in Paris, they all returned to Vancouver in 1923.

It was the Bakers' 45-year-old Chinese houseboy Wong Foon Sing who first sounded the alarm on July 26, 1924. According to him, he and Janet Smith had been alone in the house that morning, working at their respective tasks in separate areas of the home. Around noon, while Foon Sing was peeling potatoes in the kitchen, he heard a loud noise he initially thought was a car backfiring. But the noise seemed to come from the basement, so he hurried down to investigate and that was when he discovered Smith lying on her back on the floor of the laundry room. She had blood oozing from a wound over her right eye and was dressed in her usual nanny uniform—a blue denim dress with white stockings and shoes. Beside her lay a .45-calibre revolver. Wong immediately contacted Frank Baker, who rushed home, inspected the scene and then called the police.

At the first coroner's inquest, the two doctors who examined Smith's body testified that it was unlikely a single bullet would have caused the damage found in her skull. They also discovered burn marks on her torso and an unidentified stain on her left index finger.

The Point Grey police, who were initially called to the house, had for some reason found nothing suspicious about Smith's death and ruled out calling the death a homicide. It was determined that Smith had either committed suicide or had accidentally shot herself.

But the entire scenario was highly suspect. The crime scene had been botched from the beginning. Many obvious clues were either overlooked or covered up by the police, and a thorough search of the basement appeared never to have been done. Why would Janet Smith have been using a gun in the first place if she had indeed accidentally shot herself? And if it was a suicide, why had she killed herself?

Within days, many other Shaughnessy Heights nursemaids disputed the coroner's inquest verdict that Smith had committed suicide. They all stated adamantly that Janet Smith was a happy-go-lucky girl with an untroubled life and had no reason to kill herself. She was known to sing as she went about her work and the nickname "The Scottish Nightingale" was coined to describe her. In fact, some other workers in the neighbourhood came forward stating that at about 10:30 on the morning in question, they had heard Janet singing. Her behaviour was hardly the action of a girl who was about to take her own life.

It was about this time that rumours began to circulate throughout the neighbourhood, some suggesting that Smith had been murdered, perhaps even raped, by a member of Vancouver's high society, and worse, that police officials had been bribed to cover up the crime. But if the rumours were true, how could this have occurred with Wong in the house?

Some people suggested the murder might have taken place elsewhere, possibly at a high-society party the night before at the McRaes' Hycroft Mansion, and that her body was moved to the Osler Avenue residence where her death was made to look like an accident. Again, this scenario seems far from likely in view of the clothing Janet Smith was wearing when her body was discovered and the fact that she probably wouldn't have been invited to the party.

On September 9, a second coroner's investigation was held, and this time the jury ruled that Janet Smith had been murdered by person or persons unknown. Speculation continued both in Canadian and British newspapers, but after six months, no arrests had been made. It seemed the little Scottish Nightingale had been forgotten. She had become an all-too-familiar cold case.

The following March, the case took a bizarre turn—one that left a bad stain on BC's racial history. On March 20, 1925, while working on the front lawn of the Baker house, Wong Foon Sing was kidnapped by a group of vigilantes dressed in the hooded apparel of the Ku Klux Klan. He was apparently taken to an attic in a house in Point Grey where he was shackled to the floor and subjected to several beatings, death threats and other means of torture to force him to tell what he knew about Janet Smith's murder. Foon Sing refused to give in to his torturers and was released from captivity nearly two months later.

Late at night on May 1, Wong was found wandering along Marine Drive in a state of delirium. The police took him into custody and, for reasons unknown, decided to charge him with the murder of Janet Smith. He was then shipped off to Oakalla Prison to await trial.

To most reasonable people, the murder charge seemed absurd. Even the Attorney General at the time, Mr. A.M. Manson, told a newspaper reporter that he believed the houseboy was completely innocent of the crime. Manson added that he assumed the arrest had been made in order to possibly expose the real murderer. Although his statement convinced the grand jury to release Wong for lack of any substantial evidence, it still seemed Wong was being used as a scapegoat because the police had botched the initial investigation.

Common sense seemed to momentarily prevail on June 17 when kidnapping charges were laid against Point Grey reeve (mayor) J.A. Paton, Police Chief Hiram Simpson and four of his constables. In addition, three Canadian Detective Agency men who worked for the municipality were also charged for their involvement in what appeared to be a cover-up of the crime and possibly Wong's kidnapping.

None of the accused contested the charges against them, but Paton added that the whole kidnapping affair had been organized and sanctioned by the Attorney General himself. He claimed Manson had even met and discussed the kidnapping with a Point Grey representative while Wong was still being held in captivity.

Although Manson adamantly denied these accusations on the floor of the legislature, his political career was damaged beyond repair. Anyone associated with him was also smeared by the media of the day. Any aspiration Manson had to become BC's next premier was lost.

The three Canadian Detective Agency men who had been working on the case for the city received prison sentences. The charges against Paton, the police chief and the Point Grey officials were all dropped.

Rumours continued to circulate that summer concerning the Janet Smith affair, especially in the British tabloids. By then it was definitely thought that bribery, drug smuggling and political interference all factored into the case. Especially prevalent was a rumour about the immoral behaviour of the rich and powerful in Vancouver.

It was suggested in the press that Janet Smith was merely an innocent victim inadvertently caught in the middle of a violent romantic quarrel between Jack Nichol, the playboy son of lieutenant-governor W.C. Nichol and Lucille McRae, another daughter of Alexander McRae. Some people believed Lucille might have struck Janet in a jealous rage that caused Smith to slip on the wet basement floor and fracture her skull on a pipe.

The fired gun was a red herring to make her death look like suicide. Or the argument and consequential murder could have happened at the party at Hycroft Manor—described as an orgy by some people—and Smith's body was then moved to the basement of the Baker house. It was even suggested that Jack Nichol himself was responsible for Smith's death, but this theory was later disproved because he was out of town at the time of her murder.

There were also rumours, said to have come from London's Scotland Yard, that Frank Baker had operated a drug smuggling ring in London between 1920 and 1923. His own involvement in Smith's death then became suspect. Under questioning, Baker admitted that his export company had handled heroin, cocaine and morphine on occasion, but he denied ever storing drugs in his brother's house and said that Janet Smith knew nothing of his business affairs.

Poor Wong Foon Sing had simply been the victim of gross racial tensions in Vancouver at that time and had been an easy mark to take the fall for Smith's murder. The Chinese community demanded answers, as did the Scottish community who all wanted justice for Janet.

Despite witnesses who testified at the second inquest that Janet was scared of Sing, her diaries proved otherwise. Just three days before her death, a diary entry stated, "Sing is awfully devoted. He gave me two rolls of film for my camera, also sweets, and does all my personal washing and ironing."

These were hardly the actions of a man who planned to harm the young woman.

Nonetheless, it seemed that justice was not to be had. In March 1926, Wong Foon Sing decided to leave Canada and returned to China.

Three possible scenarios remained, none of which could ever be proven. One theory claimed Frank Baker had murdered Janet Smith because she had discovered his drug dealings and threatened to expose him. The second theory held that Janet had been raped and murdered at a party the night before and her body brought back to the Osler house to confuse the investigation. And third, perhaps Smith had simply been the innocent pawn in a passionate argument between two members of Vancouver's high society. But the question remains that if she had been murdered elsewhere, how could she have taken care of the Baker child on the morning of July 26 as verified by Wong?

Because the crime scene had been totally botched by the police—intentionally or by accident—and because Janet Smith's body was embalmed almost immediately after her death on the orders of a Point Grey police officer (possibly the police chief himself) with no autopsy having been performed, nothing could ever be proven.

No one, however, thought that Wong Foon Sing had been involved, as it was confirmed by many other witnesses that he and the little Scottish Nightingale always got along well and enjoyed one another's company. It was generally believed he was merely the scapegoat in an unexplainable crime.

Janet Smith's murder remains one of BC's most puzzling unsolved crimes.

In September 1925, a tombstone for Janet Smith in Mountain View Cemetery, paid for by the Scottish societies and many other anonymous donations, was unveiled before a crowd of more than 4000 people. The tombstone's broken top signifies an early death, and the following words are engraved on the stone: "On Earth, one gentle soul the less; in Heaven one angel more."

Chapter Seven

The Death of Doukhobor Leader Peter Verigin

~

On the evening of October 28, 1924, 65-year-old Peter Vasilievich Verigin, the undisputed leader of the many Doukhobors in Canada at that time and known to his followers as "The Lordly," boarded a Canadian Pacific Railway (CPR) train at Brilliant, BC, the headquarters of his empire. He was about to travel on business to Grand Forks, some 140 kilometres west. He was seated in car 1586.

Verigin was accompanied by his current young companion, 20-year-old Mary Strelaeff. Other passengers on the train included John McKie, the newly elected MLA for Grand Forks, and several other Doukhobors who were part of Verigin's entourage.

At approximately 1:00 AM, soon after the train had passed through Farron between Castlegar and Grand Forks on the remote Kettle Valley Line in southeastern BC, a powerful explosion shattered the quiet night. Car 1586 was blown to smithereens.

Doukhobor leader Peter Vasilievich Verigin, 1912

Of the 22 passengers in the car, 19 were killed or injured, more than half of whom were thrown clear of the train. Lordly, minus one leg, was found some 15 metres away. He lay dead next to John McKie. Among those who died that night were W.J. Armstrong, a North Vancouver commercial traveller; Harry Bishop, a popular Nelson athlete and businessman; Peter J. Campbell of Sand Point, Idaho, a businessman and representative for the Bruce Campbell Lumber Company; H.K. Fawcett, a Vancouver-based news agent; Murray Neil, a Grand Forks rancher; Haakum Singh, an Indo-Canadian labourer; and Mary Strelaeff, Verigin's companion.

An explosive device was first suspected, which was thought to have been placed directly beneath Verigin's seat. Another theory suggested the gas used to heat and light the car might have accidentally caused the blast, but naturally the CPR disputed this suggestion. The railway preferred to believe that either a miner travelling on the train had been carrying some dynamite that had accidentally ignited or a bomb of some kind had been used to cause the explosion. If a bomb was the cause of the explosion that killed Peter Verigin and many of his followers that night, then obviously it was an assassination of the most malicious kind.

Peter Verigin had led his people for many years with the motto, "Toil and a Peaceful Life." His nickname "The Lordly" had come about because his followers considered him to be their Lord. He was revered as a semi-deity. His "empire" covered thousands of acres of land spread over three western Canadian provinces, and his words were listened to and even studied by the politicians of the day as well as his followers. He was considered an aristocrat and an inspiration to many people, but some resented his power, and Verigin had many enemies.

Since the arrival of approximately 7500 Doukhobors from Russia to Canada in 1899, some dissident movements had grown up within the community, and by the 1920s, all were a challenge to Verigin's leadership. His first problem was the Independents who resented the fact that Lordly restrained them somewhat. They wanted their own individual prosperity, and when this was discouraged, many of them left the commune as a result.

There was also a group called the Zealots, who later became known as The Sons of Freedom. This group chastised the Independents who had abandoned the basic principles by accumulating their own individual wealth. As a result, The Sons of Freedom began burning the threshing machines and any other signs of progress made by the Independents. By the 1920s, these radicals were attacking far bigger targets, such as schools and even Verigin's own home in Brilliant. As the years went by, the radical acts of The Sons of Freedom grew in magnitude and destruction.

Even some of Verigin's closest followers who managed his vast empire were growing skeptical of the way matters were being conducted within the Doukhobor community. They were as interested in material gain as their leader—as long as he also supported their needs.

By 1924, Verigin's followers were beginning to have doubts about whether their leader was really looking out for their best interests. Verigin's constant co-operation with Canadian government laws was thought to be an act of treason to the Doukhobor principles of practicing pacifism and vegetarianism. When Verigin accommodated Canadian political authority, his followers considered this a conflict. And those who lived under the harsh conditions of Doukhoborism often resented Lordly's exalted status.

By far the biggest problem for Verigin, however, was his own son, Peter Petrovich Verigin, who had been raised in Russia by Lordly's ex-wife. Peter visited Canada in 1905 when he was 25 and had openly criticized his father as being a "crook and a bandit, a liar and a cheat." He referred to him as an "old reprobate who was only interested in young girls." No one had ever dared to say such things to the Doukhobor leader, and a few months later, Peter was ordered to return to Russia in disgrace.

It was believed that before leaving, he threatened to return one day and kill his father. Years later, in the 1960s, the RCMP had investigated this son/father theory thoroughly but could find no evidence that Peter Petrovich was involved in his father's death. Nonetheless, following the senior Verigin's demise in 1924, the Doukhobor community in Canada sent for the younger Verigin and asked him to leave Russia and become their supreme Doukhobor leader, an offer he eventually accepted in 1927. In the interim three years, he had been imprisoned in Russia by the Bolshevik authorities for his hooliganism and abuse of alcohol. However, he remained the Doukhobor leader in Canada until his own death in 1939.

So, that night in October 1924 when The Lordly boarded the train to Grand Forks, he had many enemies who might have wished him dead, despite an equal number of followers who loved and revered him.

In addition, one other person might also have had an interest in seeing the leader dead, but for a far more vindictive reason—jealousy. Anastasia Holobova had long been considered Peter Verigin's "wife," although the two were never legally joined in marriage and merely lived as a common-law couple. Anastasia was just 18 when the two first met, and she became The Lordly's favourite and constant companion. She accompanied him on all his travels to Doukhobor villages in Saskatchewan from 1902 onwards. She even travelled to the United States with Verigin, and between 1906 and 1907 returned to Russia with him.

Anastasia might have had a motive to kill her lover that night, fearing that she now had a rival for his attention in Mary Strelaeff who was on the train with Verigin. Some said Mary was simply his secretary and nothing more, but this was disputed by those who knew that few Doukhobor women had the benefit of an education at that time. It was far more likely that The Lordly's interest in young Mary was something more personal.

The train explosion was a tragedy of immense proportions, especially considering that the principles of the Doukhobors were to encourage the equality of all people and living life in a simple, peaceful manner, free of violence. The reason the Doukhobors had originally left Russia was to escape tyranny and to establish a utopian communal lifestyle where violence was explicitly rejected.

Verigin had been immersed in Doukhobor beliefs since he was a child. His early spiritual beliefs were Christian-like, and many early Doukhobors called themselves Christians and believed that Christ was the first Doukhobor. Peter had enormous leadership potential as a young man and had been groomed for that position and given daily instruction by the Doukhobor leader in Russia, Lukeroa Kalmakpova. Six weeks after her death, Peter Verigin was proclaimed leader.

But Peter had many rivals in Russia, and he was eventually arrested for sedition and acts of treason. Without the benefit of a trial, he was condemned to exile for five years, which was extended to 15 in far distant Siberia. This long hardship merely strengthened the young man, and in 1902, the authorities allowed him to join his brethren in Canada who had escaped in 1899.

With a limited education, Peter Verigin had triumphed over adversity. During his incarceration, he had been in contact with the great author Leo Tolstoy, who had inspired him.

Verigin proved to be a dynamic, wise and skilled leader in all practical matters from farming policy to religion. He was also a talented poet who wrote many psalms and prayers. He believed, as did many of his followers, that he lived a true Christian life.

Some people think that the truly great people in the world have the gift of premonition. Whether or not this is true is debatable, but some days before his death, Verigin told Anastasia, "They're writing me a letter. The devils have been watching me a long time, wanting to kill me. I've met and parted with everyone."

It is not known whether Peter Verigin did in fact ever receive such a letter, but he certainly received many threats on his life.

Shortly before he took his final journey that October evening, he had invited many of those closest to him to share a final drink with him. He then distributed nuts and raisins to the children who were always present at his arrivals and departures. Did he have a premonition of impending death that night?

Simon Kamenchikoff, a self-proclaimed Czar of Heaven, who was often seen wearing a halo of oranges on his head, had warned Peter of his possible death. He was questioned at length after the train explosion as it was thought he might know something of the plot to kill the leader. He told authorities that he had merely written to Peter earlier because of a dream he had had in which Verigin was working in the fields with many others. Verigin was stooping down as he worked and when he stood up, his face was covered in mud. Kamenchikoff asked him if he had been hit and, if so, who had done it. In the dream, Verigin supposedly cried out in despair, saying, "A strange country did this to me." This letter from Kamenchikoff might have been the one he referred to when speaking with Anastasia.

So was the explosion accidental or was it a planned assassination? Many theories were put forward through the coming years. One theory suggested the Canadian government had organized the assassination to rid the country of the volatile, outspoken man. Another theory was that the American Legion and the Ku Klux Klan from Oregon had arranged the Doukhobor leader's death because they feared he would transfer his pacifist commune (thought by the United States to be communism) to Oregon, and this prospect outraged them.

Intensive investigations into the train incident both by provincial police and the CPR came up with nothing substantial. The government offered a reward of $2000 for information leading to the arrest and conviction of the perpetrator of the crime, again with no leads.

But had a crime been committed? Was it simply a tragic accident, or was it a pre-planned assassination orchestrated by one or more of many possible suspects?

Nearly 90 years later, speculation is still ongoing concerning Peter Verigin's death.

Chapter Eight

No Justice for Molly

~

On the evening of January 18, 1943, snow was already threatening the night sky as Anita Margaret (Molly) Justice stepped off a crowded bus on Douglas Street near Swan Lake in Saanich, Victoria. She was on her way home from work. Sadly, she would never arrive.

The 15-year-old girl worked as a seamstress at General Warehouse Limited, a garment factory. She had dropped out of school early in order to go to work and help out her family financially. Molly was described as a happy girl, mature for her age, who loved her job and family. She lived on Brett Avenue with her mother, the widowed Muriel Justice, her 18-year-old brother Robin who was employed at McLennan, McFeely & Prior Ltd., and D'Arcy Martin, the man who would later marry Muriel.

Molly's mother had her daughter's supper waiting for her that night, as she knew what time Molly would be catching the bus (5:50 PM from downtown) and how long it would take her to walk home from the bus stop on Douglas Street. As the evening passed, Muriel assumed there had been transit problems and that Molly had decided to eat in town before heading home, which she had done on previous occasions.

The bus driver later stated that he remembered seeing the young girl leave the bus at her regular stop near Swan Lake and heading off into the darkness. With Canada's participation in World War II, regulations were in force for a stringent ban on all lights. Despite the darkness, and even though she did not like walking along the more remote route home, Molly took the short cut that night because she was anxious to get home quickly. She had planned an outing with her mother and brother later that evening. After leaving the bus at her usual stop, she walked along Douglas Street to Vernon Avenue and then headed down the embankment to the railway tracks that ran close to her home on Brett Avenue. Molly was carrying two parcels with her, one containing a pair of used shoes and the other a man's sweater that she had apparently purchased as a gift for her brother.

On that particular crisp January evening, many Saanich residents had been skating on nearby Swan Lake. Arthur Logie, an off-duty Saanich firefighter, and his wife were watching the skaters while on their after-dinner walk. At about 9:00 PM, they headed home, taking the narrow footpath alongside the Canadian National Railway (CNR) right of way. Arthur's toe suddenly caught on something as he kicked at the falling snow and he bent down to see what it was. He saw two parcels and picked them up. His wife suggested they take them home as they probably belonged to someone and they could see them better in the light at home. To their horror, the couple noticed the parcels were covered in blood. Arthur and his wife stared in shock at what they had found and immediately contacted the police to report their gruesome discovery.

Within minutes, Sergeant Eric Elwell and Constable Victor Smith of the Saanich Police arrived at the lonely intersection of Darwin Road and the CNR where Arthur had agreed to meet them. The three men scoured the area with flashlights and within 30 minutes found the lifeless body of Molly Justice face down in the snow, her coat and skirt pulled over her head. They estimated she had died only a few hours earlier as her body was still warm.

A guard was left at the scene while Molly's body was taken to a nearby funeral parlour and examined. It was discovered that Molly had been stabbed multiple times with a short-bladed pocketknife. Two large bruises on her head suggested she had been struck with a blunt, heavy object. There were no initial signs she had been raped.

It was confirmed that she had been stabbed more than 20 times; eight of the knife wounds were to her throat and face. Massive blood loss from her throat wounds was determined to be the cause of death. The Justice family was notified and D'Arcy Martin arrived to officially identify the young girl.

It was an enormous tragedy. Although people were by then accustomed to hearing of the deaths of young men and women far away on the war front, the death of a young, innocent girl so close to home left the community reeling.

Molly Justice had been born in Chemainus and had moved to Victoria with her mother and brother when she was seven, after her father's death. She had attended Cloverdale School but did not complete her schooling because she wanted to work and contribute to her family's income. She was a likeable, pleasant and popular young woman both at school and with her work colleagues. She did not appear to have any enemies.

Pathology examinations in 1943 did not have the benefit of DNA testing or other, more advanced mechanisms for helping reveal the identity of a killer. For example, the hair found beneath Molly's fingernails would today have been analyzed for DNA and a sole fingerprint lifted from the contents of her purse, which was found later, would have been entered into a database to search for a possible match.

The police force did the best they could with what little they had at hand. Unfortunately, the falling snow that January night covered much of the available evidence and made it more difficult to capture the perpetrator of that evil crime. In addition to Saanich detectives working on the case, the Victoria City Police, RCMP members in other areas of BC as well as naval patrol and Army Provost Corps officers helped in the investigation.

Molly's funeral was held on February 9, 1943, but the police were no closer to finding her killer. After four weeks of frustrating and meticulous work, the police finally got a break. A pair of men's gloves was found near the murder scene. It was determined that 96 pairs of that particular style of glove had been sold in Victoria between October and December 1942. The fully lined gloves were tan in colour and made of soft calf-skin with close-fitting elastic wrists circled by two coloured bands. One glove had faint bloodstains on it.

The gloves received a lot of attention in the media as the police tried to interview every single owner of the gloves. Out of 1700 interviews, police managed to clear 30 glove owners. By early March, 81 pairs of the gloves had been tracked and the owners eliminated as suspects.

Then in May, something happened that seemed to solve the case once and for all. A man wielding a knife threatened to rape an 11-year-old girl walking in the vicinity of Swan Lake. She claimed the attacker, who lured her away into the bushes, told her to keep quiet or she would end up the same as Molly Justice. The young girl later identified her assailant from police photographs as being 15-year-old Frank Hulbert, also known as Frank Pepler. He was arrested later that day and two weeks later was charged with the sexual assault.

However, while Frank Hulbert was being thoroughly inter-rogated, he claimed he was not Molly Justice's killer and instead implicated a fellow workmate: 49-year-old William Mitchell. Mitchell, a former RCMP officer, worked with Hulbert at a Victoria paint factory. Hulbert maintained that Mitchell had confessed to him that he had murdered Molly Justice.

On June 15, 1943, William Mitchell was arrested and charged with first-degree murder. A bloodstained knife was seized from his rooming house. At his trial some months later, co-worker Lewis Kamann testified that Mitchell had been working alongside him on the night of Molly's murder and both had left work late, which meant that Mitchell would not have had time to be in the Swan Lake area when Molly was killed. In his own defence, Mitchell claimed he had cut himself with the knife and that the blood found on it was his own.

The jury believed both Kamann and Mitchell, and William Mitchell was finally acquitted in the fall of 1943. In November, Frank Hulbert confessed that he had murdered Molly Justice, but he was "in a fog" about the actual event.

In January 1944, Hulbert, under the auspices of the Juvenile Delinquent Act, was sent to the Industrial School for Boys at Oakalla Prison on the mainland for the attempted rape in May 1943.

Over the next few years, he admitted on several occasions that he had been responsible for Molly's murder, always adding that it could not and never would be proven. But for some unknown reason, Hulbert was never charged.

It was rumoured that this strange turn of events had been allowed to happen because Frank Hulbert's stepfather,

Eric Pepler, was BC's Attorney General from 1934 to 1954. It was suggested Eric had intervened in the case and had always refused to release documents that were labelled "confidential," which could have contained the evidence necessary to convict Frank Hulbert of Molly's murder.

The case was again brought up for review in 1967 as a result of Molly Justice's sister-in-law Marjorie, who was still seeking justice for Molly. In October of that year, Frank Hulbert was also charged with perjury for his original testimony against Mitchell. He was convicted of the offence in March 1968 and sentenced to five years in jail. A few days after his conviction, he told an undercover police officer that he might have killed Molly because "I was the only one there."

Although a Court of Appeal ordered a new trial on the perjury charge, Crown prosecutor Wally Anderson refused to charge Hulbert with Molly's murder. On January 24, 1969, Hulbert was sentenced to a further four and a half years on the perjury charge alone.

More than 20 years later, a judge's report dated August 31, 1996 (officially called "A Review of the Conduct of the Criminal Law Enforcement Authorities, 1943–1996") dismissed the earlier theory of a murder cover-up as having no basis. Judge Martin R. Taylor's thorough investigation into the case found no conclusive evidence that a family kinship ever existed between Frank Hulbert and Eric Pepler, and no proof that Pepler had intervened in the Hulbert case.

The so-called family tie between the two men (either a nephew or stepson) was disputed, and the relationship was thought to be far more obscure. A marriage certificate of Thomas Pepler, Frank Hulbert's *real* stepfather, states Thomas was born in Toronto of unknown parents and "left an orphan as an infant." Eric Pepler was about a year younger than Thomas and was the son of an Ontario lawyer educated at Upper Canada College and Osgoode Hall. If there was a relationship between Frank Hulbert and Eric Pepler, it was a very distant one—Hulbert had simply tried to cash in on the name connection.

All the major players in the tragic death of Molly Justice in 1943 are now dead. Eric Pepler died in 1957, and Frank Hulbert died at the age of 68 in February 1996 in Port Alberni on the west coast of Vancouver Island, where he had been living for years in a converted bus/trailer. William Mitchell died in November 1961.

The surviving members of Molly Justice's family have tried to move on. Marjorie Justice passed away in 2007, and her son believed his mother's feelings "were put to rest." He stated at that time, "There is no real source of justice ever going to happen, because the fella has passed away himself now."

Subsequent generations of the Justice family still live in Victoria, some very near to Swan Lake where the murder of their relative happened so long ago. The Molly Justice case is still officially open and remains one of the oldest unsolved cases on Vancouver Island. It is also one of only four unsolved murders in the district of Saanich, the others being that of pregnant teenager Cheri Lynn Smith in 1990, Bobby Johal in 2003, and realtor Lindsay Buziak who was stabbed to death in an empty house in Gordon Head in 2008 (her story is told in a later chapter).

Most people today still believe Frank Hulbert was responsible for Molly Justice's death, but no one could ever successfully prove it in court. As a result, an innocent teenage girl never received the final justice she so rightly deserved.

Chapter Nine

Marguerite Telesford—A Morning Jog Ends in Tragedy

~

Coincidentally, exactly 44 years to the day of Molly Justice's murder, another young woman also died violently.

Early in the morning on Sunday, January 18, 1987, a pretty, 20-year-old, black University of Victoria student set off on her usual early morning jog in the area of Mount Douglas, just outside the city of Victoria. Although Telesford and Justice had no connection, January 18 proved to be a fatal day for both young women.

Marguerite's routine jogging route took her from the house she lived in on Cedar Hill Road west along Mount Douglas Cross Road to Blenkinsop Road, then north toward the intersection with Royal Drive. She would then head east along the road through Mount Douglas Park and then south again back home along Cedar Hill Road.

She always set off around 7:30 AM on her morning jog. If someone had been tracking her morning habit, its regularity might have been her downfall. On that particular cold January morning, someone was watching and Marguerite disappeared, never to be seen again.

Marguerite was born on July 14, 1966, in Porto Spain, Trinidad, and was lodging in Victoria with Bill and Norma Cowell, her guardians, while attending university. Her biological father lived in Montréal. She was a popular student and had many friends both at school and at Hillside Centre mall where she worked.

Her disappearance that morning led to a two-year investigation of mammoth proportions that turned into a roller-coaster ride for the Saanich Police Department. Even though Marguerite's disappearance and obvious murder eventually led to an arrest, a conviction and a 25-year sentence for her killer, the young woman's body was never found. How did all this happen?

Notification of Marguerite's disappearance in January 1987 happened swiftly because, on earlier runs, she had always returned home at the same time; it was unusual for her to be late. Within hours, police were combing the neighbourhood. A number of people had recalled seeing Marguerite jogging in the area on other mornings. Two people even claimed to have heard gunshots early on the morning of Marguerite's disappearance.

Everyone living in the vicinity of Marguerite's regular jogging route was investigated, and for weeks neighbours feared for their safety and that of their loved ones. Was there a serial killer on the loose? Was it a premeditated murder committed by a stalker? Had Marguerite been innocently run down in a hit-and-run accident by a motorist in the darkness of early morning? Had the motorist removed her body in a panic? And because the disappearance had occurred on Martin Luther King Day, was there a possibility this was a hate crime? The questions seemed endless as the tips kept flooding in to the police. But no concrete picture emerged of what had happened. The only evidence of possible foul play the police had in Telesford's disappearance was a pool of blood and bloodstained earmuffs found in the 1100 block of Mount Douglas Cross Road.

Four days after the disappearance of Marguerite Telesford, the Central Saanich emergency dispatch centre received a call from an obviously distressed person at about 11:30 PM, but the caller hung up before any information could be recorded. Four minutes later, another person called, who sounded even more distraught. The unknown person did not leave a name or a location, and the brief conversation was never released to the public. The caller seemed troubled about something and was urged to call either the Saanich police or Crime Stoppers. No further calls were received. An explanation was never found for the call or whether it was even connected to the Telesford case, but every incident was investigated in the event that there might have been a connection.

The original 15 investigators on the case were eventually reduced to four. Meanwhile, consultations were held with the FBI Behavioral Analysis Unit headquartered in Quantico, Virginia, to develop a profile of the unknown suspect.

Hundreds of people helped scour the Mount Douglas Park area for clues. Nearby Elk Lake, Beaver Lake and places in Sooke were also searched. Every licence plate seen in the area was checked out. Students, friends and neighbours were cross-examined in numerous interviews, and a reward of over $11,000 was posted for any information on the Telesford case. Nothing new was gleaned from these investigations. The case was slowly turning cold.

One year later, on January 11, 1988, two Saanich police officers, Barry Peeke-Vout and Michael Chadwick, were assigned to the case. By that time, a mountain of evidence had accumulated, and the two sergeants admitted to being "overwhelmed and consumed" by the enormity of the task.

Peeke-Vout commented: "It was a jewel of a case to be involved in. It encompassed just about every facet of detective work possible and at times we felt as if we were living out a plot put together by the fiendish mind of a best-selling detective story writer."

One incredible fact that only came to light a year later was that back on February 18, 1987, just one month after Marguerite Telesford's disappearance, a man named Scott Ian MacKay had been arrested by Constable Stockman at a beach in Oak Bay and charged, in the company of two other men, with the sexual assault of Joanne Gratto, a black prostitute. At the time, MacKay's vehicle, a 1975 Ford pickup, had been seized and examined before being released again to its registered owner, Darlene Metz, who was then MacKay's common-law partner.

A vital clue that would later tie MacKay to the Telesford case was a blue pompom from a tuque that was found wedged underneath the truck between the frame and a crossbar, just behind the passenger compartment. Together with other pieces of evidence from the truck, the pompom was sent to a forensic lab in Vancouver on March 13, 1987, for analysis.

Numerous items were examined at the lab, including hair, clothing and other objects found in MacKay's truck that had been stolen from other vehicles. When the lab report came back to Victoria, it was so long and detailed that the vital piece of information tying the pompom and one hair allegedly belonging to Telesford was overlooked.

Scott MacKay was interviewed again in June 1987 at the Vancouver Island Regional Correctional Centre (VIRCC), where he was serving time for the earlier sexual assault of Joanne Gratto, for which he had been found guilty. However, his denial of committing any other crime, plus Darlene Metz's statement that he was home at the time of Telesford's disappearance, provided MacKay with an alibi and failed to prove the possibility of his involvement.

Then, in April 1988, four months after new officers were assigned to the Telesford case, police were informed that at least five of Scott MacKay's jail mates from the VIRCC had stated that MacKay admitted to the murder of Marguerite Telesford. By then, MacKay was serving a 12-year sentence for various other offences.

On Wednesday, April 20, 1988, after months of intensive police work, 25-year-old Scott Ian MacKay was charged with the first-degree murder of Marguerite Telesford. Coincidentally, his trial began on January 18, 1989, two years to the day of her disappearance. Telesford's body, however, had still not been found, and the only evidence the Crown had to link MacKay to the crime was the incriminating pompom from her tuque found beneath his truck. Other evidence included blood-stained earmuffs, pools of congealed blood, hair, a 12-gauge shotgun shell and a pry-bar that was found within hours of Marguerite's disappearance at what was later confirmed to be the murder scene. There was also the testimony of five other criminals, but the Crown prosecutors wondered how reliable they could be in court.

An 11-man, one-woman jury was empanelled, and the Crown prosecutors (Dennis Murray and Diane Turner) and defence counsel (Gary Kinar) began to argue over the admissibility of certain evidence. The trial judge was Justice David Hinds, and the trial was expected to last for approximately two weeks.

The prosecution's theory was that MacKay had accosted Telesford as she jogged along an isolated stretch of Mount Douglas Cross Road. Then, having been rebuffed by her, he ran her down with his pickup truck. Murray and Turner theorized that he then shot her twice and drove off with her body, with the pompom from her tuque wedged beneath his truck.

It was later revealed that MacKay might have known Telesford and had been watching for her that particular morning. Both MacKay and Telesford had worked for Gray Line Bus Lines during the summer of 1986, but it could not be positively proven they were at work at precisely the same time or knew one another.

The courtroom was crowded to capacity every day of the trial, and the newspapers were equally brimming with all the latest court drama. Up to 120 people had crammed the benches and lined the aisles since the beginning of the trial. The courtroom had seats for only 60 people. At one point, the court was so packed that loud speakers were set up in the hallways outside the courtroom so that the overflowing crowds could listen to the proceedings. This was the first time that a trial had ever been broadcast outside the courtroom, but the judge requested the loudspeakers because the overcrowding in the courtroom had created a fire hazard.

On Monday, January 23, 1988, 33-year-old convicted criminal Danny Cain took the stand, telling the court that while incarcerated with MacKay in the VIRCC, MacKay had admitted to him that he had murdered Marguerite Telesford and had later begged Cain to help him "get off" the first-degree murder charge.

Cain's own criminal history was definitely questionable. Since 1971, he had been convicted numerous times for offences such as armed robbery, escaping custody, breaking and entering, theft and unlawful confinement, but he nonetheless announced to the court, "Holding back information regarding something of this nature isn't the right thing to do. I don't believe, knowing what I know, that this person should be walking around in society and doing the things he did."

Until that point in the trial, MacKay had remained silent, but during Cain's testimony he made two loud and angry outbursts. Throughout the four hours Cain was on the stand, MacKay stared angrily at him. When the prosecutor questioned Cain about the so-called "code of morality" that prison inmates lived by, MacKay interjected by saying, "Except for him."

Cain agreed that inmates who testified against other inmates were usually labelled "rats" or "stool pigeons" and ran the risk of physical violence from fellow inmates. Mr. Justice David Hinds then asked Cain to speak up, and again MacKay interjected: "He can't speak up because he's lying."

Cain also told the court that he and another inmate tried to talk to MacKay to see if he knew the whereabouts of Telesford's body.

"If he knew where the body was, we'd be able to negotiate something with the police," he told the jury, to which MacKay had replied (according to Cain), "You guys have got to understand, they won't have much on the case—it's all circumstantial evidence. There's only one case in history where there's been a conviction with no body found."

Cain claimed that MacKay told him that if the body was ever found, something on it would connect him to the murder. According to Cain, MacKay admitted to having sent the police on a wild goose chase to various places where he said her body was buried, including Colwood, Beacon Hill Park and even under the landmark Mile Zero Sign.

More inmates testified in court and all had similar stories. The fifth inmate, Gerry Chatten, told the court MacKay had thrown him up against a wall and said if Chatten wasn't careful, he would do to him [Chatten] what he "did to her." Chatten believed that the "her" in question was Marguerite Telesford.

Chatten said the reason he had come forward, like Cain, was because "a young girl who had a right to live and undoubtedly one day wanted to have children, a future...was denied that chance unnaturally." He strongly believed it was his duty to testify.

One of the inmates said that MacKay offered him $5000 to give perjured testimony stating that other inmates were conspiring to pin the murder on MacKay.

Was there any honour among thieves? Not as far as MacKay was concerned. He simply believed that his prison mates had all conspired against him. When MacKay took the stand, he asserted that convicts Perry Mandzek, Michael Smith and Gary Chatten had testified simply to confirm Danny Cain's testimony. Furthermore, MacKay believed that another inmate, Michael Walsh, who had once been his former bridge partner at the VIRCC, testified against him only to get the reward money for information leading to his arrest.

When Darlene Metz, MacKay's common-law partner, took the stand, she claimed MacKay had not left their home on Prior Street the night of Telesford's disappearance. She admitted it was possible, but she did not hear the truck start. Generally, she woke up if she heard the truck.

Crown prosecutor Dennis Murray asked her, "But there may have been times when you slept through the truck starting?" To this she replied, "There may have been."

However, under cross-examination by MacKay's defence counsel, Metz said the possibility of MacKay leaving the house without her knowing it was as likely as "beings from another planet landing in Sooke."

Metz claimed she and MacKay were playing cards the night before at his parents' home on Sooke Road and had returned to 2610 Prior Street around 12:30 AM. She said she went straight to bed but couldn't say for sure whether MacKay did too. She knew that when she woke up between 8:30 and 9:00 AM on

January 18, he was there watching television. MacKay had parked the truck in its usual place when they had arrived home the night before, and the truck was in the same place when she awoke. A second vehicle, a Honda Civic, was also at the home.

Although the couple had been having problems in their relationship, Metz said both she and MacKay had pruned trees in their backyard on the afternoon of January 18.

Darlene Metz's brother, who had lived with the couple between January 1987 and February 1987, admitted to seeing shotgun shells in the kitchen drawer of MacKay's home and said he and MacKay had once taken a gun-safety course together.

Another witness, Victor Skinner, who had worked as a roofer with MacKay in 1986, told the prosecutor he and MacKay had gone trapshooting once in 1986. At that time, MacKay had borrowed a 12-gauge pump shotgun from his father. When Skinner was shown the pry-bar found at the alleged murder scene, he confirmed it was a tool used by roofers.

Scott MacKay, wearing a pinstriped suit and tie, confidently took the stand and despite the damning evidence against him, insisted that either his prison mates or the police had framed him. He vehemently denied that he had ever admitted to killing Marguerite Telesford and stated his fellow prisoners had only testified against him in order to claim the reward money.

He stated either the police or Danny Cain had planted the pompom on the undercarriage of the pickup. The pompom, however, had been returned to Marguerite Telesford's guardians one year after her disappearance, so the prosecution, in cross-examination, asked MacKay: "Is it your evidence that the pompom with a negroid hair found in the undercarriage of the pickup is part of Danny Cain's plot against you?"

MacKay responded that he thought either the police or a friend of Danny Cain's had put the pompom there.

"Any idea how one of Danny Cain's friends could have got into the Cowells' house (Marguerite's guardians) and got the tuque with one of Marguerite's hairs on it?" the prosecution asked MacKay.

MacKay retorted that the police had placed it there in order to frame him for the crime.

Jimmy Page, another inmate, testified with some startling evidence. He said that in 1979, Cain had testified against another inmate in exchange for a reduced sentence. Page told the court that Cain had told him he had a good thing going. In fact, Cain said he had "a better deal going than robbing banks." He figured if they got MacKay, they would get "30 big ones," in reference to the amount of money to be made. At this rate, he had insisted, he would be out on the street in 18 months.

Page added that in his opinion, the court was making a mockery of the justice system by parading all "this scum" through court. He said it was an insult to all the good people of Victoria and especially the dead girl.

So, what was the truth? Were the inmates lying? Was Danny Cain just a con artist making money on the side for drugs and deals with the police to reduce his own sentence?

On this high note, Gary Kinar decided to close for the defence. Another inmate had been scheduled to testify but had decided not to at the last moment.

Everything was then set for both the prosecution and the defence to give their final submissions to the jury. Then the jury would decide the fate of Scott Ian MacKay.

After final submissions, the judge instructed the jury on various points of law. They were to be sequestered under heavy security and would not be allowed to listen to the radio, watch television, receive any newspapers or talk to anyone outside of the jury until they had reached their verdict.

On February 2, 1989, the jury was sequestered in a hotel to deliberate. During the 16 hours of deliberation, the jury requested MacKay's criminal record be read to them. It was a long list dating back to 1980.

Finally, on February 3, the court reassembled. The jury had reached its verdict: guilty of first-degree murder.

MacKay, looking thin and wearing black wire-frame glasses, a tweed sports jacket, jeans and boots, was described by the judge as being an incredibly dangerous man who had an appetite for sexual violence. At the time of Telesford's disappearance, he had been out on bail from the previous sexual assault charge on Gratto and for unlawful confinement charges stemming from that same 1987 incident.

Before being escorted out of the courtroom by five security personnel, MacKay's last words to the court were, "I'm not guilty."

MacKay was sentenced to life in prison with no possibility of parole for 25 years. His lawyers immediately appealed the verdict, which was said to be "unreasonable and not supported by the evidence." Kinar maintained the search of the pickup truck was contrary to the Charter of Rights and Freedoms. He also argued that many other mistakes had been permitted in the trial, including allowing MacKay's past criminal record to be read into evidence.

The appeal was denied, although his conviction was reduced to second-degree murder. The sentence, however, stood, and MacKay was to be locked up for 25 years, with the possibility of a parole hearing after 15 years.

In 2004, a parole hearing did take place, at which time Scott MacKay was said to "have no memory" of the murder whatsoever. His memory lapse did not further his case and certainly did not bode well for an early release.

In August 2008, MacKay's lawyer at that time, Mel Hunt, re-examined the earlier appeal because he claimed that, "DNA tests ordered after the appeal showed that hair found at the 1987 murder scene of 20-year-old Marguerite Telesford didn't belong to his client." Hunt's re-examination of DNA evidence had come about because a murder conviction in Manitoba had been overturned. That prompted BC's Criminal Justice Branch to re-examine all cases dating back 25 years in which, "microscopic hair analysis played an important role in obtaining a conviction."

At the time of this writing, MacKay remains in prison. He is not eligible for another parole hearing until 2014.

A thorough search for the body of Marguerite Telesford, including draining a holding pond behind the Lilydale Poultry processing plant on Sooke Road, had initially been conducted but her remains were never found. This fact alone makes the case unique.

~

The disappearance of Marguerite Telesford was just one more mysterious occurrence in the Mount Douglas Park area. Over the years, many other tragedies have occurred on or around the mountain, including suicides and motor vehicle accidents.

The mountain's history dates back to 1859 when Governor James Douglas set aside an area eight kilometres northeast of Victoria for parkland in the Mount Douglas area, then known as the Hill of Cedars. From 1889 onwards, the mountain and its surrounding parkland were protected as Crown Trust land,

and in November 1992, the land was officially transferred to the municipality of Saanich.

Today, the Mount Douglas area is one of Greater Victoria's most prized beauty spots where trails are lush with an abundance of ferns and wild flowers, and towering Douglas fir and cedar trees. From the summit of the mountain, a lookout offers a 360-degree view of rural Saanich, the city of Victoria and both the Olympic and Cascade Mountain ranges.

Despite its beauty, the area of Mount Douglas holds many mystical and magical legends and secrets, some of which, like the disappearance of Marguerite Telesford, have yet to be fully explained or resolved.

One story involves a First Nations man named Tanas Johnny back in the 1860s who believed he had seen a devil snake or sea devil rise up before him in the vicinity of the mountain. It might have simply been a camel that had strayed from a pack imported into Victoria on their way to the Cariboo area. Whatever he saw caused him to have a fatal heart attack.

During the 1870s, flakes of gold were found in a piece of quartz on the slopes of the mountain, subsequently making it the site of BC's third gold rush. Today, two mine shafts remain at the intersection of the Harrop and Whittaker trails on the western slope of the mountain.

In 1942 Victoria artist Emily Carr was in Vancouver visiting her friend, Ira Dilworth, when suddenly she had a vision and felt compelled to return immediately to Victoria, sensing that the forest at Mount Douglas had something important to tell her. Her subsequent paintings created in Mount Douglas Park during August of 1942 were the last of her spiritual communions with nature before her death in March 1945. However, she had managed to vividly transpose onto canvas so much of the magic and mystery of the forest. Emily Carr was only one of many people who have felt a spiritual connection to the forest throughout the decades.

Hopefully, wherever Marguerite Telesford rests today, she is able to feel that same spiritual peace and connection to nature.

Chapter Ten

The Unsolved Murder of Lindsay Buziak

~

On February 2, 2008, a beautiful, vibrant, 24-year-old woman was found dead in an empty, newly constructed house in a middle-class residential neighbourhood of Victoria.

Her name was Lindsay Buziak. She was a real estate agent who, earlier that day, had received a phone call from a woman with a foreign accent asking Lindsay to show her an upscale home in the 1700 block of De Sousa Place in the Gordon Head area around 5:30 PM that evening. The unknown woman appeared eager to buy the home that same day.

Later that day, Lindsay received a second call from a man who said he would be the one meeting her at the house. Lindsay was somewhat concerned about the two calls and had an uneasy feeling, but she agreed to meet the prospective buyer or buyers at the appointed time, as it could be a profitable sale for her. But something still seemed strange about their request to view the home, so she allegedly called her boyfriend, Jason Zailo, also a real estate agent, and asked him to meet her later at the house.

Around 6:15 PM, her badly mutilated body was discovered in an upstairs bedroom of the home at De Sousa Place. She had been stabbed multiple times.

Two calls were made to the police to report the crime, one from outside the home asking the police to check on Buziak and another from inside asking for medical help when Buziak's body was found. Initially, the police refused to confirm Zailo made the two calls. Two people, one being Zailo and the other a friend of his, had arrived at the house soon after 6:00 PM to check on Lindsay. Zailo admitted that when he arrived, he had called Buziak from outside the home at approximately 6:15 PM. When she did not answer, he called the police. The front door was locked and he could not enter at first, but when he looked through the window, he could see Lindsay's shoes inside the hall, so he knew she must be inside. Eventually, Zailo and his friend were able to enter the house through a back door. It was Zailo who allegedly found Lindsay's body in an upstairs bedroom.

The neighbourhood was in shock as the police investigation began. The real estate community feared the murder was targeting all female agents showing houses alone. Was the murder a warning? People's fears were soon put to rest when the police confirmed that Lindsay's murder was not a random killing. She had been specifically targeted by a killer or killers unknown.

On February 6, Jason Zailo returned to the crime scene with the police and his lawyer in tow, and a videotape of him walking the officers through the home was made. Much later, in 2010, the video was shown on NBC TV's show *Dateline*.

From the moment the police tape had gone up around the entire house and across the cul-de-sac at De Sousa Place, the media had become more and more obsessed with the brutal, inexplicable killing, and the story grew to gargantuan proportions.

That's when the theories and conjectures surrounding the murder began and the many "armchair detectives" talked constantly about what might or might not have happened. Naturally, Lindsay's boyfriend was initially a prime suspect, as was his mother, an ex-boyfriend and anyone or everyone connected to Lindsay's past. The public believed there were far too many unexplained questions. Was she involved in drugs? Gangs? Had her killing been a "hit" of some kind? All these questions were thrown around and speculated upon. But the murder was a violent one—not indicative of a hit—and it resembled a crime of passion.

The public seemed to forget that a family was mourning the loss of a beloved daughter, sister and friend. Lindsay's uncle, Art Reitmayer, acted as the family's spokesperson in order to answer media questions. He confirmed the family was satisfied with the police investigation to date and that much of the speculation had to be disregarded to enable the police to continue following up on reliable and substantial clues rather than mere conjecture or hearsay.

On February 9, the family gathered for Lindsay's funeral at St. Andrew's Cathedral in Victoria. At that time, Lindsay's father, Jeff Buziak, pleaded for anyone who knew anything to come forward. His pain and anger over his daughter's murder were clearly apparent, and he was determined to bring the killer to justice.

On February 12, having searched the condo where Buziak and her boyfriend had lived, the police gave their last press conference about the case, stating no more updates would be given while they continued with the investigation. They also asked the family not to speak to the media.

The police had already rejected many of the theories being thrown around. Jason Zailo, his mother and an ex-boyfriend were all exonerated, but that did not stop the suspicions and unanswered questions that still lingered.

A year later, when the crime was still no closer to being solved, despite the police's intensive work of interviewing more than 1000 people and delving thoroughly into Lindsay's past both in Victoria and in Calgary, more information was released. An eyewitness provided a description of the two people who had allegedly arrived to see the house at De Sousa Place, and a police artist made a sketch of them that was released to the public.

One of the individuals was described as a blonde female, 35 to 40 years of age, who was dressed in a white, black and red/pink dress in a large striped or colour-block pattern. She was accompanied by a male described as a Caucasian with brown hair, approximately six feet in height and of medium build who was well dressed and wearing a light- or medium-brown jacket.

But even the police sketch seemed bizarre. There was no clear description of the man, and the sketch of the woman showed a strange-looking profile. In addition, the outfit worn by the woman would not have been suitable attire for a cold February day, and it seemed an odd choice of clothing if one was intending to commit a murder. Such a distinctive outfit would have stood out. And why had a whole year passed before this information had been released to the public? People began to wonder if the police knew more than they were saying. Had the police in fact already identified the murderer or murderers but urgently needed one more piece of evidence to confirm their suspicions?

And even though the TV special that aired in 2010 on NBC's *Dateline* provided a re-enactment of the murder, it failed to generate any positive leads.

Throughout it all, Jeff Buziak, who lives in Calgary, remained prominent in the media, arranging walks and vigils on the anniversary of his daughter's death in support of finding her killer or killers. His determination was admirable.

BC Crime Statistics

Perhaps because of its geography and location in Canada, in the province of BC, crime is big. In May 2008, the following statistics came to light. There are an estimated 20,000 marijuana grow ops across the province, many of which are well hidden in the mountains and valleys of the interior. It is estimated that the marijuana industry yields revenues of $5 to $7 billion per year. More than $1 billion worth of cocaine has been seized at the borders—an amount that more than tripled from the previous two years.

British Columbia is the main port of entry for chemicals used in the manufacture of drugs such as methamphetamine and ecstasy. Asian gangs in the province are the largest suppliers of ecstasy within Canada and the U.S. And did you realize that in 2008 there were roughly two dozen gang-land slayings in Vancouver alone?

The number of homicides in the lower mainland was nearly three times that of Toronto. And 11 of the top 20 most dangerous cities in Canada were located in British Columbia, with the number of operating gangs functioning in BC having jumped from less than 10 a decade ago to 129 in 2008.

It is then no surprise that BC has become a key hub for organized crime. Unfortunately, it would seem that the business of crime is most definitely booming.

A "Find Lindsay Buziak's murderer" page on Facebook was created that was followed by many users. It also allowed the armchair detectives another place to post their opinions and theories on the crime.

Lindsay's mother, Evelyn Reitmayer, who lives in Victoria, kept in the background, quietly mourning her daughter. No parent should have to bury a child, and Evelyn had no wish to expose herself to even more pain by constantly talking to the press.

Meanwhile, Lindsay's entire family resented the many rumours being circulated about Lindsay and her lifestyle. Jeff Buziak insisted his daughter did not do drugs, despite reports to the contrary. She had earlier spent time in Calgary and her name had been connected to a known drug dealer there who, a short while before her murder, had been busted for possession of the largest ever cache of cocaine in Alberta.

In February 2010, two years after the murder, the Greater Victoria Real Estate Board and the Canadian Real Estate Association (CREA) joined with the Buziak family to post a $100,000 reward for any information that would solve the case. The reward was open for six months in the hope of renewing the public's focus on the murder. The police also released more information at that time, stating that the cell phone used to contact Lindsay Buziak on the day of her murder had been registered in Vancouver and activated in the name of Paulo Rodriguez. In addition, police announced they were still seeking information on the couple who were allegedly seen arriving at De Sousa Place. More leads were followed up in Vancouver, Calgary and Washington State, but no progress in the case has been reported.

The third anniversary of Lindsay Buziak's murder has now come and gone, and the case remains unsolved.

The house Lindsay was trying to sell was still on the market a year after her death, listed at $949,900. The price had only dipped $16,000 from the original listing price of $964,900. The house remained a tough sell. Despite subsequent changes in price, the house has not been sold.

Certain facts in the case remain clear. Lindsay was most definitely lured to this particular high-end property for the specific reason of killing her; she was not randomly targeted. The public relations officer for the Saanich Police Department believes her homicide was carefully set up by her killer or killers, and luring her to an empty house was part of that evil plan. The police don't know why she was murdered, and without a motive, it has been impossible to tie the whole case together and make an arrest.

There will never be complete closure for Lindsay's family, but bringing the perpetrators of this unspeakable crime to justice would certainly help. The police believe someone out there knows what happened or at least knows something that would help them in their ongoing investigation.

"Lindsay was intentionally targeted, she was intentionally lured to the home and she was intentionally killed," stated Saanich Police spokesperson Sergeant Julie Fast, in February 2010.

Fast's words still ring true. And her killer, or someone close to him or her, also knows those words to be true and what actually happened that day.

Anyone with information about Lindsay Buziak's death, should contact the Saanich Police Department at 250-475-4356 or Greater Victoria Crime Stoppers at 1-800-222-8477.

Chapter Eleven

The Highway of Tears

~

A young Aboriginal girl is walking alongside a highway in northern British Columbia. She hears a vehicle approaching and turns. She raises her thumb in a hitch-hiking gesture. The vehicle slows down and pulls over. The girl leans toward the driver's window. Words are spoken and the girl gets into the vehicle. She is never seen again.

That same disturbing scenario has happened many times during the 1970s, '80s and '90s. The girls were almost always Aboriginal and were between 14 and 20 years of age. Often the occurrence ended up with the discovery of a discarded body. But more often than not, the young women simply disappeared off the face of the earth and are still missing today.

This road is Highway 16, a section of the Yellowhead Highway in northern British Columbia, first given the number "16" back in 1942. But today, in the 21st century, with so many reports of women disappearing, the 800-kilometre section of the highway between Prince George and Prince Rupert has become known as the Highway of Tears. An obvious and disturbing pattern has emerged and continued through the years, causing the authorities to wonder if a serial killer was, or is, at large.

The actual number of murdered or missing women in that area dating back to 1969 is unknown but is believed to be around 43. At least 18 of those cases show alarming similarities and are believed to be linked; the women might have been victims of the same killer.

Families in the area today are trying to enforce a law that would make hitchhiking illegal. However, much of the Native population in the vicinity is impoverished and cannot afford a vehicle and no other transportation is available. Hitchhiking to get from one place to another became the only option for these young women.

In March 2006, some non-profit organizations established a list of recommendations for increasing the overall safety of the area, including a shuttle bus system, emergency telephone booths on parts of the highway without cellular reception and implementing a program that educates parents to be more aware of where their children are and where they are going. This program has made some progress and has been partly funded by the government to the tune of $52,000. But was this a case of too little, too late?

The murder of Monica Ignas, aged 15, is believed to have been the first recorded case of missing women along Highway 16. She disappeared east of Terrace in December 1974 and her body was later found in a gravel pit. In 1988, a 24-year-old woman, Alberta Williams, was found murdered a month after she disappeared. By 1994, the disappearances and murders of young women were increasing at a rapid rate.

That particular year, three victims were discovered. Ramona Wilson, 15, disappeared while hitchhiking to a friend's house in June, and her remains were found a year later near the Smithers Regional Airport. Five months later, Roxanna Thiara, also 15, went missing near Prince George and was later found dead near Burns Lake. The remains of yet another 15-year-old girl, Alishia Germaine, were discovered in December.

The RCMP is now officially investigating the unsolved murders or disappearances of nine women between the ages of 14 and 25 since 1974. Most of these women were hitchhiking along the Highway of Tears. At least eight of these cases have similar modus operandi.

For example, both Ramona Wilson and Roxanna Thiara had left their homes and were assumed to be hitchhiking to meet a friend when they went missing. Another young girl, 16-year-old Delphine Nikal from Telkwa, who was also last seen hitchhiking, disappeared somewhere between Smithers and her home. Her body has never been found.

Lana Derrick, age 19, was a forestry student in Terrace who was last seen at a gas station before disappearing in October 1995, never to be seen again.

For the next seven years, no other cases were reported. It has been speculated that the killer might have been serving time in jail during that period for an unrelated offence.

Then, a young woman named Nicole Hoar, the first Caucasian victim, disappeared on June 21, 2002. She had been tree planting in the area and was on her way from Prince George to her sister's home in Smithers. She had hoped to attend the Midsummer Music Festival, but she never arrived.

Nicole's family and friends quickly spread the story to every possible major news outlet by starting a large missing persons poster campaign and offering a reward for information to help find their loved one. More than 200 volunteers, with help from airplanes and helicopters, searched for Nicole, but to date she remains on the list of missing women along the Highway of Tears.

On September 17, 2005, several ceremonies were held in communities between Prince George and Prince Rupert to "Take Back the Highway." Local speakers came to voice the horror of what was happening. Marches and prayer vigils were organized promoting awareness of the violence being perpetrated against these innocent young women.

But the tragedies continued. Tamara Chipman, 22, went missing a few days later. She was a young woman proficient in the art of judo and would have been able to take care of herself if she were attacked. Her heart-broken father has walked the highway many times, searching frantically for his only child. She was never found.

More names were added to the list of victims as the years progressed. Crystal Lee Okimaw, 24, vanished from Prince George and has never been found. A 14-year-old girl, Aielah Auger, who was reportedly last seen getting into a black van, was later found dead on the side of the road.

All of these missing or dead women were last seen while travelling along or near the infamous highway.

The police decided to put together a profile of the type of person preying on these women. It was thought the killer might be a well-dressed travelling salesman who would seem trustworthy and honest at first glance. He might be a hunter who frequents the area and then disappears for a while after each murder. Or he could be a truck driver who travels the highway on a regular basis. The perpetrator of these horrific crimes could also be someone who actually lives and works in the vicinity and is known to locals.

In August 2009, it was suddenly announced that the police were combing a five-acre property at Isle Pierre in rural Prince George. They had received a tip about the remains of Nicole Hoar, the young tree planter who had been missing since June 2002. The property had once been owned by Leland Vincent Switzer, who was serving a prison sentence for shooting and killing his brother in 2002. The police also searched the property for other missing women. The owners of that property were not under suspicion, although the police were definitely interested in Switzer, who in December 2005 was finally convicted of his brother's murder.

More details on Nicole Hoar were also released, such as the clothing she was wearing at the time of her disappearance between June 21 and June 23, 2002. She was dressed in capri pants, sandals, a tank top and a red shirt with a yellow collar and the word "Ravens." She was carrying a dark green bag with an orange patch on it, as well as a large purple backpack.

The search of the property put hope in the hearts of the victims' families that at least one of the disappearances would be resolved, but the search came up empty. No human remains or any other evidence were located on the property.

Two more years have now passed, and the disappearance of the young women along the Highway of Tears has yet to be explained or solved. Meanwhile, the investigation continues.

THE MYSTERIES

The dictionary defines the word "mystery" as "something that cannot be known, understood or explained." In other words, it is a puzzle or a conundrum. Hopefully, the following five stories will arouse your curiosity and make you wonder what really happened.

The first unexplained mystery concerns the righting of an old wrong involving the discovery of a feng shui site that finally established the existence of a "lost" cemetery site. The second story is about a miracle birth on a magical night in the wilderness of Indian Arm. Also included are some unexplainable occurrences on the West Coast as well as a story about a painting that kept changing for no apparent reason. The final mystery is a heart-breaking story of the disappearance of a four-year-old boy more than 20 years ago.

Will we ever be able to fully comprehend these mysteries? Will answers ever be found? Or will they remain lost forever in the mists of time?

Chapter Twelve

A Rediscovered Feng Shui Site

~

Back in the 1890s, the Lake Hill area of Saanich in Victoria near Swan Lake was pure wilderness, mainly home to wildlife. In this idyllic location, a few farmers also lived and worked on the land they had cleared.

In 1891, the Chinese Consolidated Benevolent Association (CCBA) of Victoria had legitimately purchased land in the area, as well as land on the southern slope of Christmas Hill, which was designated to be used as a cemetery because it contained good feng shui (pronounced in English as "fung shway"). The Chinese only bury their dead on sites with worthy feng shui, and the CCBA had gone to great lengths to find suitable land with feng shui in that particular area.

The farmers who were blissfully cultivating their land back then were strongly opposed to a cemetery in the vicinity, especially if it happened to be a Chinese cemetery. Racial prejudice was so rampant at that time that a member of one particular farming family was said to have stated in horror that "one day along came some Chinese with a coffin and a body in a wagon for a burial on land which was adjoining ours—and we were determined to stop this from happening." The farmers were so incensed that they armed themselves with shotguns and drove the Chinese people away, forcing them to seek another site for burying their dead.

Because a stalemate continued to exist between the CCBA and the farmers, an arbitrator stepped in to settle the problem. It was decided the property purchased by the CCBA had to be sold and another site found for the Chinese cemetery.

In 1902, one of the annoyed farmers, George Hicks, purchased the property from the CCBA for $925, after which the association purchased an alternative site with good feng shui at Harling Point in Oak Bay, another suburb of Victoria. By 1903, the CCBA established a cemetery on that site. However, the Chinese community did not forget the unfairness of the deal and ill feelings simmered for several decades.

The mystery behind this story is that for many years no one ever knew the exact location of the first proposed cemetery or, in fact, if a cemetery on the site had ever really been planned. Despite extensive investigation by historians wanting to know the truth, the mystery remained. Some wondered if the whole ordeal was merely an exaggerated story passed down through generations. Perhaps there had never been a feud between the farmers and the Chinese over the placement of a burial ground.

Years later, Dr. David Chueyan Lai, a professor of geography at the University of Victoria, in collaboration with the CCBA, developed a feng shui model to trace the exact location of the cemetery originally proposed on the Lake Hill land purchased by the CCBA in 1891. He did so by following the exact principles of feng shui. This method enabled Lai and the CCBA to prove the story was true.

By following that model, they discovered the site must have been "flanked on the east by Lake Hill (called the Green Dragon) and on the west by a lower ridge (called the White Tiger)." It was backed by Christmas Hill, named "the pillow mountain," and was to have faced a small hillock known as "the Desk Mountain" and an expansive plain known as "the Grand Hall." This symbolic feng shui site was linked to Swan Lake, known as the Luminous Pearl, and it met all the required criteria. Once the model was established and the site confirmed, Saanich council agreed that a sign should be placed on the site to honour the land and to right a long-time wrong.

On Sunday, April 22, 2006, Saanich mayor Frank Leonard, together with members of his council, officiated at a sign unveiling the first official feng shui site in Canada. The ceremony took place a short distance from the Saanich Municipal Hall, along what is known as the Galloping Goose Trail, overlooking Swan Lake. The location chosen for the sign was particularly significant as it marked the culmination of Dr. Lai's work and celebrated the Chinese culture by righting an injustice against the Chinese people at a time in history when different cultures were not tolerated, recognized and honoured as they are today.

A sign that marks the "First Official Auspicious Feng Shui Site in Canada";
Swan Lake in background

~

The unveiling ceremony was an auspicious event, commemorated with dragon dancers and speeches describing the importance of the ancient traditional Chinese belief representing thousands of years of living in harmony with nature. Feng shui involves geographical, philosophical, mathematical, psychological, aesthetic and astrological concepts relating to both space and energy and applies not only to burial sites but also to the way people choose where they live. It seeks to "improve the human condition through the manipulation of physical space in a way that will impact on its corresponding qualities in humans."

It is believed the term "feng shui" originated in the *Burial Book* written by Guo Pu in the Jin dynasty. In the 19th century, the Chinese government published various almanacs containing charts, diagrams and numerical data to be used in the practice of feng shui.

Naturally, cynics continue to criticize the practice of feng shui, declaring it to be a form of superstition and merely a conglomeration of rough guesses at nature to which fanciful and immature diagrams are added. However, feng shui principles remain deeply rooted in ancient and traditional Chinese beliefs. The original masters of feng shui were hired by the early emperors of China before any war—it was believed they had the power and knowledge to manipulate the wind, water and fog, and were subsequently able to direct the outcome of battles.

In the Western world today, those ancient beliefs have more credence. It is said that even famous people such as Donald Trump and Prince Charles have consulted feng shui models at some point in their lives before making an important decision.

In any event, the official existence of this particular feng shui site in BC has now become a sign of respect for ancient Chinese beliefs.

Close-up of the sign that marks "The First Auspicious Feng Shui Site in Canada"

~

And, in the process, the mystery of a long-ago proposed cemetery has been solved, and a racial wrong has been made right in order to achieve harmony with the environment by the proper placement and arrangement of space.

Chapter Thirteen

Woman from the Mist Performs a Miracle

~

In 1911, a young couple named George and Meg Dayton became the new managers of the Wigwam Inn at Indian Arm, BC. The hotel was approximately 40 kilometres from Vancouver at the mouth of Indian River on Indian Arm, just north of Burrard Inlet. The Daytons' employment might well have been considered nothing out of the ordinary, except for two rather remarkable factors concerning Meg.

To begin with, the Daytons were not a typical couple. Meg, although still in her early 20s, suffered from a chronic arthritic condition that caused her to limp badly and to be in considerable pain most of the time. But that didn't stop her from working hard alongside her husband. When they answered the newspaper advertisement for a position at the inn, Meg convinced her husband that they would be chosen, and they were.

The other reason the couple was atypical was because of the extraordinary, somewhat surreal event that took place during their time at the hotel. It's a story that involved the rustic wilderness retreat, Meg's courage and strength and a wrinkled old Native woman who performed a miracle, one that no one has ever been able to explain or understand.

The history of the Wigwam Inn dates back to 1906 as the dream of Benjamin (Billy) Dickens, a Vancouverite originally from Ontario. Dickens was also the founder of the first advertising agency in Canada and had long envisioned building a luxury wilderness resort that would cater to the rich and famous. He already had a location in mind: at the head of the north arm of Burrard Inlet where fishing and hunting were excellent and the mud flats were full of clams. Unfortunately, his rather elaborate building plans ran into a few financial snags along the way.

In 1910, well-known Vancouver resident and millionaire Gustav Constantin Alvo von Alvensleben, the son of a former Prussian ambassador, believed in Dickens' dream and invested in the project. The money from von Alvensleben, some of which was rumoured to have come from Kaiser Wilhelm himself, gave Dickens the help he desperately needed to build his resort.

By June 1910, the inn was ready for its grand opening, and the developer, now known as the Indian River Park Development Company, chartered the steamer *Baramba* to sail up the Arm with 600 people aboard. All were anxious to inspect Dickens' newly completed luxury inn.

Advertisements for staff were placed in Vancouver newspapers. The Daytons answered the ad asking for managers.

After an interview, the couple was chosen for the job. Meg's younger sister, Emily, and her father also joined the couple at the inn in order to help with the chores.

The Wigwam Inn, now with a strong German theme rather than First Nations' one as its name implied, played host to many important people in those early days. Among the guests was a young Joachim Ribbentrop, who later became Adolf Hitler's foreign minister. John D. Rockefeller and John Jacob Astor were also among the inn's early guests.

Meg Layton was popular with everyone. She always carried out her tasks with a smile despite her pain. She was a courageous woman who had been born in Wales but had come to Canada initially to help her arthritic condition. Her left arm had been kept in a splint and her hip was badly diseased. Always interested in hotel work, she had soon found a job as a cashier with a Canadian Pacific Railway hotel and later moved to the Leland Hotel in Kamloops, where she met and fell in love with farmer George Dayton who had a milk contract with the hotel. By April 1911, Meg's condition improved, although by no means was she cured. Despite her affliction, Meg, with the assistance of her father and Emily, was able to fulfill all her obligations that summer.

By September, the hotel was officially closed for the season, but Meg and George were asked to stay on as care-takers during the winter months. Meg's sister and father also remained behind.

The Wigwam Inn, where a miraculous birth took place in 1912

~

In October, Meg and Emily took a brief trip to Vancouver for Meg to have her regular medical check-up. Sadly, Meg's arthritis had not improved, but much to her amazement, she discovered she was pregnant and the baby was due the following April. Meg and George had been told many times that it would be impossible for her to have a child, so when Meg returned to the inn and told George he was to become a father, his first concern was for his wife's health. He wanted them to leave the isolated inn immediately and return to Vancouver where good medical help would be nearby during her pregnancy. She had been told that her arthritic hip might lead to complications during delivery.

Meg was convinced that as long as she followed doctor's orders concerning diet and exercise, she would be able to stay at the inn through the winter months. To appease her anxious husband, she agreed that they would leave Indian Arm at least a month before the baby was due. George reluctantly agreed they would stay until March.

The winter months passed uneventfully, and by February the weather had begun to turn spring-like, allowing Meg and Emily to take daily walks along the nearby trails. The two sisters enjoyed these excursions, but on February 22, during one of their walks, Meg slipped on the wet ground, lost her balance and fell, hitting her head on a rock as she went down.

Emily was panic-stricken. She ran screaming back to the inn to alert George and her father, but by the time they reached Meg, she was already sitting up, rubbing her head and wondering what all the fuss was about. George immediately ordered his wife back to bed but, apart from the scare the family had received, Meg seemed to be okay.

Meg went into premature labour that night. It was a full two months before her due date, but her fall had obviously hurried things along.

There were no telephones at the inn so any communication with the outside world was impossible. Greatly distressed and fearing for his wife's life, George decided he would go to the nearby Buntzen Lake logging camp where a doctor was in residence. Even so, it would mean a long, arduous journey down Indian Arm by boat, followed by a hike inland from Buntzen Bay toward the lake.

Meanwhile, Meg's father tied towels to the bedpost for Meg to pull on each time she had a contraction while Emily patted her sister's forehead with a cool cloth and tried to comfort her.

In near pitch-black darkness, George set off on his mission to find a doctor. Once he reached Buntzen Bay, he left the boat and stumbled through the darkness toward the inland lake, helped momentarily by the appearance of northern lights that lit up the dark sky as though in answer to his fervent prayer for guidance. But the journey was to no avail because when he reached the camp, he was told that the doctor had left for a few days. George phoned Meg's Vancouver doctor who promised to leave with his nurse at daybreak.

Many long hours later, George returned to the inn to discover that his wife had slipped into a coma. He placed a mirror to Meg's lips to see if she was still breathing. Her three loved ones clung together, taking comfort from the fact that hopefully Meg's doctor would arrive at daylight.

Thinking to hurry the doctor's arrival by waiting down at the wharf, George rushed outside into the cold, grey dawn. A heavy fog now hung over the water in patches and, as it lifted slightly, he heard the sound of splashing water. George felt sure it could not be the doctor already, but he prayed that he and his nurse had made good time.

But what he saw was a solitary canoe manned by a wrinkled old First Nations woman. George frantically called and waved to her for help, and the woman paddled closer to the wharf, assuming he wanted to buy her fish.

The old woman was dressed in soiled navy pants and a heavy sweater, with a red bandanna on her head and a pair of large gold hoops through her ears. Her gumboots were muddy and she smelled strongly of fish, but to George she was the most beautiful person he had ever seen. He had no idea why, but something told him that this strange apparition from the mist would be the one person who would be able to save Meg.

It was soon obvious that the woman spoke no English so, as he helped her out of the boat, George persuaded her in sign language to come with him to help his wife. The woman seemed to understand and followed him to the inn. Once inside, George led her to a washbasin, insisting that she at least wash her hands as well as the fish knife she proposed using on her patient. The Native woman then took charge, ushering everyone out of the room as she began to administer to Meg.

No one knows exactly what happened next. Against all medical odds at that time, the mystery woman from the mist managed to save Meg's life. Two hours later, the baby's cry was music to George's ears.

Meg made a quick recovery, with no memory of what had occurred that night during her long ordeal, but she felt instinctively that this enigmatic woman had saved her life. The woman, according to the doctor who later attended Meg, had worked in a professional manner and seemed to have far more medical knowledge than was available at that time.

Meg squeezed the woman's hand in silent thanks and understanding. Then, in the general confusion and excitement of the moment, no one noticed that the old woman had quietly slipped away. George was upset because he wanted to thank her personally and give her something for all that she done for them.

The next morning, however, the Native woman reappeared at the inn with a handmade papoose basket for Meg's baby. After much argument, the woman finally accepted the food and money that George insisted she take. And then, once more she went on her way. She was never seen again.

Despite asking numerous people about the woman, George couldn't find out anything about her. From his description, no one was able to tell him who she was. In fact, no one had ever heard of or seen such a person in the area.

The Daytons named their daughter Marguerite, and her birth was the prelude to a rather miraculous life during which Marguerite's own courage, like that of her mother's, was brought to the forefront on many occasions. Years later, just before Marguerite's marriage, she was diagnosed with bone cancer in her right foot. She valiantly fought the cancer and beat it.

Marguerite's only daughter was born with an eye problem and needed a lot of medical attention. The exorbitant medical expenses took Marguerite and her husband years to pay off, especially throughout the Depression years.

During World War II, Marguerite took a job as a truck driver for David Spencer's Store in Victoria to help out with expenses, in addition to looking after her home, her husband and daughter and two other young children they cared for. For many years after the war, Marguerite and her husband worked at Victoria's famous Empress Hotel. The couple celebrated their 60th wedding anniversary at the Empress in the early 1990s. Marguerite later took care of her ailing husband for some years before his death. Life was not always easy and Marguerite often paralleled her own life with that of the Wigwam Inn itself.

Back in 1914 at the start of World War I, the inn was forced to close down because of its predominantly German theme, which was not popular at that time. It opened again in the 1920s with a new owner and a brand new elegance. During the Depression years, it became a day lodge, serving lunches only and selling First Nations' crafts. The building was modernized once more in the 1950s and operated as a casino in the 1960s until the RCMP brought all those activities to an abrupt end. The inn was also used on occasion for movie locations. Eventually, with a general downtrend in business, the inn fell into disrepair and sat vacant for several years. During that time, it was vandalized and many of its prized possessions were destroyed, including the inn's guest book that was found floating in the waters of Indian Arm. Only a few pages could be retrieved.

Then, in the 1970s, Arjay Developments Ltd. purchased the building and rejuvenated it. Western Pacific Resorts Inn, as the latest owners, spent a great deal of money to turn the inn back into the ultimate retreat it once was. Today, the Royal Vancouver Yacht Club owns the Wigwam Inn, but it is only used for special private events.

Two years after the inn held yet another grand re-opening in 1980, Marguerite West (née Dayton) returned to the place of her birth for the first time since February 1912. "I felt that before I died I needed to see the place my parents had told me about so often," she said.

By then, Marguerite was 70 years old, but her emotions were strong as she wandered around the area, thinking about the story of her miraculous birth so long ago.

I ambled away from the inn and walked along the trails, trying to imagine the exact spot where my mother might have fallen that day and struck her head. Then I walked down by the water's edge and pictured in my mind's eye that old First Nations woman with the magical powers coming out of the mist. I wanted to experience the immense relief my father must have felt at that moment in time. And, finally I was able to say a silent prayer of thanks for the miracle at Indian Arm which gave me life.

Marguerite West has now passed on, and today we are left to wonder what really happened on that night so many years ago. Who was the woman with the magical powers who came out of the mist, performed her miracle and then, just as suddenly disappeared again? Did she ever really exist?

The papoose basket in which Marguerite slept as a baby was definitely real. It was re-discovered many years later in the attic of the Dayton family home in Kamloops. George Dayton's sister gave the basket to the Kamloops Museum for their First Nations display, a single reminder of a miraculous event that appeared to have no medical explanation.

Chapter Fourteen
Five Marine Mysteries

~

Graveyard of the Pacific

I t is rumoured that British Columbia's coastline holds many secrets and that its waters are full of intrigue and mystery. For example, the area surrounding Vancouver Island to the south and west has been dubbed "The Graveyard of the Pacific" because of the numerous shipwrecks that have occurred there. The many storms along the coast coming in from the Pacific Ocean have obviously played a large part in these tragedies down through the decades, but why is one particular stretch along the BC coast so deadly? It's a mystery that has long plagued mariners.

The Graveyard of the Pacific is a 65-kilometre stretch of treacherous coastline off southwest Vancouver Island between Port Renfrew and Cape Beale. It is in that area that numerous ships have been lost. Some say there is one shipwreck for almost every nautical mile of water. Beneath the raging waters are more than 60 wooden sailing vessels as well as more modern, large steel freighters. Most of the shipwrecks occurred between 1903 and 1972, and hundreds of individuals lost their lives, their remains lying at the bottom of the ocean.

The power of the sea in that region has claimed ships for hundreds of years. Long ago, First Nation canoes that capsized were thought to be the first fatalities, followed by the loss of many Japanese vessels that caused fishermen to be swept out to sea and drown. More modern vessels have been wrecked by a combination of storms, fog or human error—or was it perhaps simply the mystery of the Graveyard of the Pacific at work?

Perhaps the greatest single loss was the wreck of the steamer *Valencia* in January 1906. The ship was on its way north from San Francisco to Victoria, BC, when it overshot the entrance to the Strait of Juan de Fuca and smashed into the shoreline just south of Pachena Point. With an enormous hole in her hull, the ship quickly filled with water and six half-loaded lifeboats fell into the sea, capsizing and killing at least 60 people. In total, 117 people perished in the tragedy and only 37 survived.

A later enquiry blamed human error—the captain was supposedly confused by the vessel's speed in the fierce winter storm that ensued and steered the boat off course. Others believe the shipwreck was simply another example of that mysterious stretch of water claiming its unsuspecting victims.

One positive result of the *Valencia* disaster, however, was the establishment of the famous West Coast Trail in today's Pacific Rim National Park Reserve. Initially, the trail and its cabins were specifically built to be used by shipwrecked survivors and their rescuers.

The steamer *Valencia* capsized in January 1906 when it overshot the entrance to the Strait of Juan de Fuca and smashed into the shoreline south of Pachena Point.

The entire BC coastline is rugged and stormy, but only that one particular stretch has claimed so many ships. Why? The answer remains a mystery.

The Tale of the Jumbo Squid

Another marine mystery concerns the strange jumbo squid. Finding one in BC waters used to be a rare event, but in recent years, more of these squid have been sighted or found in fishing nets all along the coastline. Since 2007, scientists have found at least 82, and they seem to be continuing to head as far north as Alaska.

Mexican fishermen call the squid *Diablos Rojos* (Red Devils) because of their vivid colour that switches from red to white as they flash underwater. The squid are often harvested for calamari and squid steaks. Because of their enormous size, it has been asked whether the squid can attack humans. No squid attacks have occurred in BC, but they have been known to nip at people in the South Pacific.

The creature's body extends up to two metres in length and has 10 appendages. Scientists claim that a squid should definitely not be toyed with because it could be a killer. Squid are known to eat whatever they come into contact with, including each other.

But why are these squid invading BC's waters when they are known to prefer the warmer waters of the south? Therein lies the mystery.

BC's "Killer Whales"

So-called "killer whales" are well-known residents of BC waters, but there are two distinctly different types. Scientists believe the two types—the meat eaters and the fish eaters—have not interbred for thousands of years. They even "squeak" a completely different language, or so it is claimed. Why they do not mix and mingle with one another is a mystery.

Although the whales share the same waters, they appear to have separated into two distinct factions. Finding a reason for this separation of whale species could unlock the mystery of the origin of the species in general.

Killer whales (the meat-eater transients) travel from California to Alaska and usually hunt in small groups. They have no predators and are known as "the wolves of the sea."

The southern resident whales (the fish eaters) navigate mainly around the Georgia Strait and Puget Sound in summer. These are the ones tourists most often see on whale-watching expeditions.

If the transients and residents ever pass each other in BC waters, they ignore one another completely and do not communicate. Their language might sound different to one another and would not be understood. The transients are quiet while the residents are chatty.

One wonders whether the difference is simply something in the genes of each whale species or whether an event many thousands of years ago caused their indifference to one another and triggered the split between the two types of whales on the west coast of North America. This event might have been a battle of sorts between the two species; a battle in which no one came out the winner. For now, no explanation can be found.

Are there Mermaids in British Columbia?

Did you know that in 1967, passengers on a British Columbia ferry heading to Swartz Bay on Vancouver Island claim to have seen a mermaid sitting on rocks at the entrance to Active Pass? She was described as having long blonde hair, and the lower part of her body was similar to a porpoise. At the time, she was said to be eating a salmon. A man in an aircraft flying above had captured her on camera and had the photograph printed. The story was reported in the *Victoria Times-Colonist,* but unfortunately none of the ferry passengers who saw the mermaid were available for further comment.

A second mermaid was reported to have existed back in the 1870s and 1880s. Three men had gone fishing with their First Nations guide off Point Grey, which is the current site of the University of British Columbia. A mermaid with long yellow hair and brown skin rose up from the water close to their boat. As the mermaid stared at the men, the guide became anxious. He claimed it was a bad omen to see a mermaid, as another man of his tribe had earlier seen one in the Squamish River, north of Vancouver, and had apparently died soon afterwards.

The Mystery of the Washed-up Feet

Another far more horrifying mystery has recently come to light along the beaches of BC. Since 2007, numerous decaying feet encased in running shoes have been washing up around the Strait of Georgia. Why has this been happening and in such a short period of time? And why is it that just feet are showing up and not other body parts? To whom did these feet belong?

Scientists from the University of British Columbia (UBC), the University of Victoria (UVic) and the Institute of Ocean Sciences are convinced the feet are from bodies that sank in BC waters. They are not likely to have been washed in from other parts of the world, such as Asia, disproving the theory they belonged to victims of the 2004 tsunami in Thailand. It is not believed the feet could have travelled that far across the Pacific Ocean.

A consensus of opinion is that the feet belonged to victims lost in the Strait of Georgia, which include the Gulf Islands and San Juan Islands, Burrard Inlet, the Squamish River and possibly even Northern Washington State. The feet that were found near the Fraser River might have come from farther north and been washed downstream. Winds and currents could possibly account for this movement.

The feet might even have belonged to people from Vancouver who were victims of some unfortunate incident such as accidental drowning or even murder. Experts claim that most human body parts lost in the ocean usually wash up close to their point of entry into the marine ecosystem. Decayed bodies in the water eventually break apart and can float in the currents for months before being washed ashore.

Perhaps the strangest part of this marine mystery is that seven of the feet that washed ashore between August 2007 and November 2008 were all wearing sneakers of various well-known brands. Two of those were Nike sneakers, and lab tests proved they belonged to the same victim, a male. One foot was discovered on February 2, 2008, on Valdes Island and the other on June 16, 2008, in Ladner. Three of the other feet belonged to males and two to females. Some were right feet and some left, but only the two feet clad in Nike sneakers were thought to have come from the same person.

Then, in October 2011, the Coroners Service of British Columbia released a report stating that two of the matching feet that washed ashore in 2008 in Richmond have now been identified and that no foul play was involved. DNA has positively identified the feet as belonging to a New Westminster woman, whose name has not been disclosed. The right foot was found in May 2008 and the left in November of that same year on a beach along the Fraser River, also in Richmond. Both feet were encased in matching size seven New Balance running shoes. Autopsies showed that the feet were probably separated due to the natural process that occurs in a marine environment.

A concrete explanation of why these human feet are suddenly being found on BC's shores has yet to be offered. Although both police investigators and scientists find this puzzling, it is also a horrible human tragedy.

Could the missing feet belong to any of the more than 2000 missing people in BC today? Maybe one day an answer will be found. Meanwhile, the enigma of where these feet came from is just one more unsolved marine mystery in the province.

Chapter Fifteen

The Changing Chilliwack Painting

~

The delicate line between illusion and reality had always fascinated artist Hetty Fredrickson. Hetty believed some mysteries were better off never being solved. The events that occurred in a Chilliwack house in which she once lived certainly tested her beliefs to the extreme.

From 1969 until 1988, Fredrickson was best known on Vancouver Island because of her Valley of a Thousand Faces Art Gallery in Sayward, a tourist attraction just 70 kilometres north of Campbell River in the beautiful Sayward Valley. Hetty and her second husband, Douglas Fredrickson, had started the unique attraction when she began painting faces of famous and infamous people on the ends of cedar-wood slabs that Douglas cut for her on their three-acre property in Sayward. Douglas was a logger, and the couple was immersed in the Sayward logging community. Hetty used cedar wood because she wanted to save money on canvases while at the same time inspiring local children to become interested in art.

Hetty Fredrickson at work on one of the many faces she painted, 1985

During those years, it wasn't just children who were fascinated by Hetty's art gallery in the woods. People came from around the world to view the intriguing faces Hetty painted on the cross-section slabs of wood she attached to the trees in the forest. Her "art gallery" also included other types of paintings, but the odd faces in the forest were the ones that intrigued old and young alike.

However, long before Hetty's artistic fame spread to Sayward, she and Douglas had lived in a 14-room heritage house in Chilliwack on the mainland, and what happened to them while living there remains a mystery to this day.

Born Hetty Mulder to Dutch parents in Tegal, Java, Indonesia, where her father was a lawyer for the Dutch government, much of Hetty's childhood was spent amid the mystical beauty of the country. At 14, she and her sister were sent back to Holland where she attended Kennemer Lyceum High School. She later moved to The Hague to study art at the Free Academy for Creative Arts for three years. Her artwork was greatly admired, and many of her paintings were sold to art collectors in Holland, Italy, France and Germany. Some of her works found their way into the private home gallery of a multi-millionaire art dealer.

When World War II broke out in Europe, and with her parents held captive by the Japanese back in Indonesia, Hetty and her sister were on their own in Holland. For the next five years Hetty lost complete contact with her family, but she led an adventurous life working for the Dutch Resistance—she was once picked up by the Gestapo and held captive for 10 days. Her fearless bravado at that time was indicative of how she led her entire life.

Soon after the war, Hetty's sister died from a mysterious illness that had first afflicted her as a baby. Now, being alone and desperately wanting to establish some security for herself and her parents, who were returning to Holland to be nursed back to health, Hetty entered into a bad marriage. It did, however, produce two wonderful sons of whom she was proud.

Eventually Hetty divorced her abusive husband and moved to Canada, where she was determined to make a better life for herself and her boys. After taking many menial jobs and travelling west from Montréal, Hetty settled in BC working as a housekeeper for Douglas Fredrickson, a logger and divorced father with three children of his own. They fell in love and in due course were married. The couple moved to Chilliwack, where Hetty established herself as an art teacher while taking care of her blended family.

And it was in Chilliwack that Hetty fell in love again—but this time with a house. She had driven by a particularly intriguing-looking house at 342 Williams Street North many times and then one day noticed a "For Sale" sign outside. She knew she had to have the house and persuaded her husband to buy it. They moved into the 1912 three-storey-plus turret home in 1966. Hetty soon set up an art studio in the basement where she conducted art lessons for young students.

The home had a great deal of charm and certainly stirred Hetty's creative juices, but strange and somewhat disturbing events began to happen in the house soon after the Fredricksons moved in. Mysterious, unexplained footsteps in the middle of the night and dresser drawers that constantly opened on their own were the first indications of a possible haunting at the old house. But Hetty was a down-to-earth person and wanted to find a logical explanation for what was happening.

She did some research on the history of her home and discovered it had once been a boarding house. Hetty also found out that a man had committed suicide in the house in the 1950s, and there had even been a possible murder. The body of a woman who, according to rumours, might have been killed, had been cemented into a stone chimney in the house. There was indeed a chimney in the dining room that had been cemented in some 30 years earlier.

These stories were mostly hearsay, and Hetty had no definite proof that anything bizarre had ever taken place in the house. However, she began to have a recurring nightmare that left her shaken and upset when she awoke in the mornings. In her nightmare, Hetty was walking up a flight of stairs leading to the attic where a woman dressed in a vivid-red housecoat with yellow flowers on it was lying on the floor. Dust was swirling around the woman and her arms were raised. Only one of her eyes was visible.

Hetty firmly believed that the woman in her nightmare was the "ghost" who had been haunting the house. Thinking as an artist, she decided the best thing to do would be to capture the "ghost" on canvas. She reasoned that if the apparition was moving around the house opening drawers, it might also move its own painting.

So, for several nights in a row, Hetty sat up in the attic waiting for inspiration, and one night she was rewarded for her patience. She saw an outline of someone standing beside the small attic window and, once the apparition disappeared, Hetty felt a strong urge to paint the scene she had witnessed so often in her nightmare. She worked feverishly until the piece was finished. Then she left the room, leaving the picture on the easel, having marked the exact spot on the attic floor where it stood. Despite checking every day afterwards, the painting never moved, and eventually Hetty lost interest in her ghost.

Some weeks later, one of her art students asked her about the ghost painting she had told them about earlier. Hetty decided to show her students the painting, and they climbed the stairs to the attic.

Hetty was aghast to find changes had taken place on the canvas. One side of the female face that she had left blank—the way the face had originally appeared to her in the nightmare—had now taken on a shape and looked more masculine than feminine. There was even a faint outline of a moustache on the face, and the frightened look was replaced by a threatening, angry glare.

Hetty felt sure there *must* be some logical explanation for the changes, so she had laboratory tests done on the canvas at the Harrison Art Gallery in Vancouver. The results were inconclusive but did prove no human hand had altered the painting in any way. Pretty soon the media got wind of the strange occurrences in the so-called haunted house on Williams Street North, and reporters began to constantly invade the lives of Hetty and her family. Everyone wanted to interview her and see the painting for themselves. On one occasion, 700 people turned up on her front lawn, breaking steps and pushing to get into the house and see the "ghost" and the painting.

Hetty decided she and Douglas should open up the cemented chimney in the dining room, but Douglas thought it would be far too expensive and probably wouldn't prove anything. A professor from the University of British Columbia, who was also a member of the British Society of Psychic Research, agreed that no purpose would be served by opening up the chimney. Even if a body was found, it would just bring more unwanted publicity to the Fredrickson family.

Hetty received numerous letters as well as a constant stream of telephone calls that made life somewhat unbearable for the family, so she decided to go to Holland to visit her mother. She took her ghost painting with her and arranged for it to be inspected by Dr. Haaff, a famous professor of parapsychology in The Hague. Haaff was unable to cast any more light on the matter other than to say he detected a distinctly spiritual influence at work on the canvas.

On a later visit to Japan, where one of Hetty's sons lived, the painting once again became a topic of great interest. In the unanimous opinion of many learned people, it was agreed that a spiritual individual was indeed trying to "come through" the canvas and speak. The painting was featured on Japanese television where it was set on a timer system to see if any more changes took place. Small changes did continue to happen.

On her return to Chilliwack, Hetty found she had become somewhat of a celebrity. Jack Webster asked her to be a guest on two open-line CKNW radio talk shows on Halloween night in Vancouver. The telephone lines were jammed throughout the whole program. One listener even asked Hetty if she was a member of the witch's union, to which she replied: "No, they require motorized brooms and I just can't seem to adjust to them." Despite the stress of the strange happenings in her home, Hetty had not lost her sense of humour.

CKNW offered to buy Hetty's canvas in order to raise money for charity. To Hetty, the painting was priceless, so instead she decided to donate it to the station in order to raise money for an orphans' fund. "I'm sure this was the first ghost in history who ever contributed money for the benefit of the living," she later joked.

After the painting was hung in the CKNW studio, further changes to the canvas began to take place. Hetty had painted a book on a table in the painting and had left the book cover entirely blank, but suddenly, four words had appeared on the book that were all clearly decipherable: "Blest," "Soul," "God" and "Prayer." It was beyond strange.

In 1968, a haunted house was built on the grounds of the Pacific National Exhibition (PNE) in Vancouver and the painting was loaned to the PNE to hang in the house. Hetty also donated furniture from the so-called "haunted attic" room of her Chilliwack home—a chest of drawers and a bed. Some time later, a fire on the PNE grounds burned everything in the haunted house—everything, that is, except for the painting. The two curtains hanging on either side of the canvas were burnt to a crisp, but the canvas was unscathed.

Meanwhile, Hetty had discovered a small room in the turret of her Chilliwack home. The door leading to it had long since been papered over. Upon inspection, Hetty found the room was completely empty but was amazed to find dust swirling around, similar to the dust she had first seen in her nightmare. The dust, however, proved to be deteriorated insulation material.

Hetty's haunted house at 342 Williams Street North, Chilliwack, after the first fire in the early 1970s

In late 1968, the Fredricksons finally decided to sell their haunted house and move to the Sayward Valley on Vancouver Island where Douglas was now working. After they left, there were two fires in the old house on Williams Street North in the coming years, the second of which (in 1975) completely destroyed the entire building.

Hetty became convinced that the haunting she had tried to capture on canvas was somehow connected to the fire. Today, another house stands on that site. Hopefully the owners of the home have not experienced any of the bad vibes from the haunted house that previously stood there.

The last time Hetty saw her painting, she noticed it had faded somewhat, but if anything, the expression on the ghostly face appeared even more severe and angry than it had years earlier. She had hoped that using the painting for good works such as raising money for the needy might have made the ghost a little happier.

Moving to Sayward led to the creation of The Valley of a Thousand Faces that brought Hetty even more fame, though of a more pleasant nature. The faces she painted ranged from the whimsical to the serious. Politicians, movie stars, Disney characters and even Big Bird from *Sesame Street* delighted the thousands of visitors who strolled through the forest every year. She maintained that her aim was to send people home with a smile, which she achieved.

Hetty Fredrickson's "Groucho Marx" painting in the Valley of a Thousand Faces, Sayward, BC

"Snow White and the Seven Dwarfs," painted by Hetty Fredrickson in the Valley of a Thousand Faces

Hetty Fredrickson's "Indonesian Man" painting in the Valley of a Thousand Faces

~

She continued to believe that nature was really too perfect to be captured on canvas. For that reason, she preferred the surrealistic and the more unusual themes, many of which depicted her own beliefs about life. One of her paintings—of an old Indonesian woman from Hetty's childhood—had a million-dollar price tag attached to it. The price said it all; she didn't want to sell it, and she knew no one would ever pay that much money for it.

In Sayward, Hetty was no longer looked upon as the "Witch Lady of Chilliwack," even though her artwork continued to favour the surreal. She also liked to experiment with other forms of art, such as the huge figure she made out of tobacco cans depicting a person crying out to the drug, alcohol and tobacco profiteers of this world. She admitted to being hooked on smoking herself though.

Hetty also created a four-metre-high depiction of a Sasquatch—an optical illusion made from weird shapes of hanging tree limbs and moss in the forest. The reflection of the sun added the required effect for the illusion to seem real.

Model of a "Sasquatch" in the Valley of a Thousand Faces, created by Hetty Fredrickson

Unfortunately, in 1988, Hetty was forced to close down her gallery in the forest because of her failing health. She sold many of her faces on the cedar slabs and for a while only displayed a few paintings in her indoor gallery along with some other artwork.

But Hetty never forgot the time she spent in her famous "haunted house" in Chilliwack and recounted that strange story many times, especially at Halloween. It made a good ghost story.

Hetty Fredrickson died in 1994 from leukemia, and the world lost an incredible talent. The truth behind her haunted Chilliwack painting remains a mystery to this day, lost somewhere in that delicate line between illusion and reality.

Perhaps Hetty was right. Some mysteries are better off never being solved.

Chapter Sixteen

The Michael Dunahee Story

~

At approximately 12:30 PM on March 24, 1991, a young boy just two months short of his fifth birthday disappeared without a trace from a playground at Blanshard Park Elementary School (now known as University Canada West) on Kings Road, near the city of Victoria.

Michael Dunahee's disappearance became one of the largest police investigations in Canadian history. To date, more than 20 years later, he is still missing and his disappearance remains a complete mystery.

On that fateful day, Michael's mother, Crystal, was getting ready to participate in a female touch-football game. His father, Bruce, was helping get the gear out of the car and Michael's sister, six-month-old Caitlin, into her buggy. Michael, who had asked on the way to the playing field if he could play on the swings nearby while his father unloaded the family car, vanished in a split second just metres away from his parents. Once Bruce noticed that Michael was no longer in the play area, he began calling his son's name, but there was no response.

Soon everyone was running in all directions searching for Michael. Within minutes, Bruce asked a neighbouring home-owner to call the police.

No one had seen anything suspicious and no one came forward as a witness to Michael's disappearance, though it was later rumoured he might have been seen getting into a brown van. Whatever happened to Michael must have occurred in a fraction of a minute. And it left a family broken-hearted with many unanswered questions.

Within minutes of his disappearance, the case had gone from searching for a young boy who might have wandered away to finding a boy who had been taken by someone. In the first two months following Michael's disappearance, the police worked around the clock searching for him. Numerous leads were investigated, including five telephone calls to the Dunahee house suggesting that a satanic cult had taken Michael. The FBI was brought on board. Posters were distributed throughout Victoria and many cities across Canada. They even reached the United States, and Michael's story was featured on *America's Most Wanted* five times, which was unprecedented. Crystal also appeared on *Oprah*, the *Geraldo* show and the *Dina Petty Show*, all of which emphasized the important issue of missing children across North America.

Any initial suspects and all possible early scenarios were ruled out. Even Michael's parents had come under scrutiny by the police, but it was concluded they had done absolutely nothing wrong. They were a caring couple whose son had simply been snatched from them while they had looked away for one second.

On a personal note, my own daughter was in grade 10 in Victoria the year Michael disappeared, and my son had already graduated and was on his way to college, but I clearly remembered the early years in which we had spent countless hours in playgrounds or at sporting events. My husband and I had watched our son play soccer while our daughter played on the swings nearby. Every parent in Victoria was now thinking the same thing—this could have been our child who was snatched from us while we looked the other way for just a moment. We could imagine how devastating life must have become for the Dunahee family. How, we wondered, could anyone survive such a tragedy and find a way to go on with their lives?

No longer were children allowed to walk to school without some kind of supervision. No longer did we allow our children to play alone. We knew predators were out there and that life would never be the same again. We all lost our innocence on that heart-breaking day in March 1991.

Twenty years after Michael's disappearance, Crystal Dunahee said in an interview that she and her family have lived "in a time capsule" ever since that horrific day. Time has stood still for her once happy family who were forever robbed of the happiness of having a son. They no longer had peace of mind. Crystal and Bruce lost their beloved son, and a sister lost a brother she never had a chance to get to know. She was a little girl who was forced to grow up in a household of sorrow.

Since Michael disappeared, the Dunahees have continually worked with the police, living in the hope that each new lead will be the one that finds Michael and brings him home. For years, Crystal kept his bedroom just as it was on the day he vanished. Birthday and Christmas presents were accumulated for his return. She firmly believes Michael is alive but, as the months drag into years, she no longer gets excited about each new police tip.

In a 2006 interview, Crystal said, "I have learned I cannot live like that. I don't want to get up on that emotional plateau where you're filled with hope and then come crashing down. I can't let myself go there anymore."

By that time, her weariness and utter despair were showing. She had become resigned to the terrible blow fate had dealt her family.

Nonetheless, Crystal and Bruce Dunahee have never completely given up hope. Crystal has become a strong advocate for missing children in BC as the president of Child Find British Columbia and as a member of the National Board of Child Find Canada. Child Find was established across Canada as a network of charitable, non-profit organizations that deliver services to families whose children go missing. The organization started in Alberta in 1983 in response to the disappearance of a six-year-old Edmonton girl. That same year, it began in BC. Since the Victoria office was established in 1991, there are now several satellite offices throughout the province because of Michael Dunahee's disappearance.

In 2002, Crystal also lent her voice in support of the RCMP to introduce an Amber Alert system in BC. Unfortunately, the parameters in place for an Amber Alert to be launched would not have assisted with the search for Michael even if the program had existed back in 1991.

In addition to working with Child Find BC, the Dunahees hold an annual charity event called the Michael Dunahee "Keep the Hope Alive Fun Run" that raises money for Child Find. The run takes place around the anniversary of Michael's disappearance and is now in its 20th year. Dances are also organized to raise funds, and a baseball Tournament of Hope is held annually. In October 2011, Crystal Dunahee was awarded the Order of BC for her ongoing work on the issue of missing children.

Through all of the agonizing years since the Dunahees lost their son, the police have followed literally thousands of leads and tips. In 2006, residents of Chase in the interior of BC were convinced that a young man who had arrived in the area in 1991 (the year of Michael's disappearance) was Michael. The story was carried prominently throughout the news. Was this Michael? Had he been abducted and grown up elsewhere with another family? Sadly, after DNA testing, the lead came to nothing. The young man was not Michael Dunahee.

Statistics on Missing Children

Missing children are usually placed in one of three categories—runaways, stranger abductions or parental abductions. Runaways and parental abductions both comprise 49 percent of the missing children cases, with stranger abductions making up the two percent, according to the caseload of Child Find BC.

There are four other categories of missing children listed by the RCMP. Child Find registers such cases and lends assistance to parents, the police or other social service agencies involved. These four are divided among "Accident" (the child is believed to have been injured or involved in some type of accident); "Wandered off/Lost" (foul play is not suspected and there is a high probability of finding the child); "Unknown" (first-time runaways are often placed in this category to begin with as are some stranger abductions, and there may or may not be reason to suspect foul play); and "Other" (when a child is missing from an institution or treatment centre).

In the 10 years between 1997 and 2007, the total number of missing children in Canada rose from 58,098 to 60,582, the largest number usually being in the runaway category.

Another young man in Port McNeil on Vancouver Island was also rumoured to be Michael but, once again, DNA testing proved otherwise.

In early 2009, yet another lead led to a possible link between Michael's disappearance and a child killer in Milwaukee, Wisconsin. A missing person's poster of Michael was discovered inside the home of 62-year-old Vernon Seitz who had confessed, just before dying, to having killed at least two children back in 1958. Again, after investigation by police, the lead proved to be false.

A $100,000 reward for information on Michael's disappearance remains in place. The police received another 550 tips following the initial announcement of the reward money, but again all leads went nowhere. In the Victoria Police Department, at least 12 filing cabinet drawers in the missing persons' section concern Michael's case. Deputy police chief John Ducker, the only remaining Victoria police officer who worked on the original case immediately following Michael's disappearance, is still haunted by that day. "Someone out there is responsible," he stated. "That someone has lived with this burden for far too long and we encourage them to come forward."

Michael Dunahee, a young, innocent boy with blond hair and blue eyes, became everyone's child on that March day in 1991. We all knew his endearing face from the thousands of distributed posters. Throughout the years since, we have watched him grow up through the technology of the age-enhancing police sketch artists' portrayal of how he might look as a 10-, 12-, 15- or 17-year-old. In early 2011, another sketch of Michael in his 20s is still being worked on.

The Dunahees have tried to move on with their life, but not a day goes by without them thinking of Michael and wondering what really happened. The best-case scenario would be that he was sold to an adoption agency and adopted into another family who had no idea the adoption was illegal. Michael, who would now be a young man of 25, might one day have a vague feeling or memory of another time, another place, another family and wonder.

Worst-case scenario—well, the Dunahees refuse to go there. Instead, they prefer to concentrate on the positive. They are convinced that one day Michael's disappearance will be solved and that he will come back to them. Miracles happen.

"It's kind of nice that the police are as stubborn as we are," said Bruce Dunahee in a 2011 interview with the *Victoria Times-Colonist*. "They don't want to give up and neither do we."

In May 2011, Crystal met with Prime Minister Stephen Harper in Ottawa on the occasion of the launch of the Canadian Centre for Child Protection (www.missingkids.ca). She continues her fight for lost or missing children and cannot imagine a time when she won't be involved. Back in 1991, there was nothing like the technology available now, but in today's world, anything is possible.

Anyone with any information about Michael Dunahee's disappearance should call the Victoria police tip line at 250-995-7444 or Crime Stoppers at 1-800-222-8477.

One day an answer to this tragic event must, and most certainly will, be found.

THE PARANORMAL
AND
THE LEGENDS

The last chapters in this book show BC in a completely different light and prove the province is not only known for its murders and mysteries but can also lay claim to other more supernatural matters.

The stories in this section are about monster sightings, some UFO tales, a few hauntings and a couple of legends. Each story illustrates that anything is possible and that nothing should ever be totally dismissed or doubted even if it can't be explained.

Perhaps not every mystical happening needs an explanation. Solutions to what appears to be the supernatural are sometimes best unknown, leaving our imaginations to simply wonder and ask—what really happened?

Chapter Seventeen

Monster Sightings—Ogopogo and Caddy

~

Other than unsolved mysteries and infamous crimes in BC, the province has also been inundated with sightings of lake monsters and sea serpents, especially in the 1920s and 1930s.

One of the most famous of these creatures supposedly lives in Okanagan Lake in the south-central interior area of the province, and another swims in the waters off Cadboro Bay near Victoria. Both monsters are related in size and description to their Scottish cousin in Lake Ness. These two particular creatures, however, have histories dating back far beyond the 20th century.

According to Salish Native legend, Ogopogo, the Okanagan Lake creature, is reputed to be a demon-possessed man who had murdered a local man called Old Kan-He-Kan, hence the name given to the lake—Okanagan. The murderer was supposedly transformed into a lake serpent as punishment for his crime and was cast into the waters of the lake for all eternity. The creature was given the name N'ha-A-Itk, which roughly translated means "creature of the water," "water god" or "lake demon."

Despite many First Nations legends concerning Ogopogo, the early white traders who came to the Okanagan area in the mid-1800s ignored these stories and were amused by the animal sacrifices made to appease the so-called "monster" and protect the Natives from being attacked.

Then, in 1872, a white woman, Mrs. John Allison, maintained she had seen the monster swimming in the lake, and she recorded the event in detail. Since then, many people have become staunch believers in the sea serpent, and there have been several sightings.

Folklore had originally told of a lair or cave under Squally Point near Rattlesnake Island (just offshore from Peachland) in which the sea serpent monster supposedly lived. For this reason, First Nations people would never paddle their canoes too near this area for fear a storm would blow up that would bring N'ha-A-Itk up from the depths to claim another life.

It was not until 1940 that N'ha-A-Itk became known by the more common name Ogopogo as a result of a familiar ditty written at that time: "His mother was an earwig, his father was a whale, a little bit of head and hardly any tail…and Ogopogo was his name."

Today, Ogopogo is viewed as a much kinder creature, with reports stating it either travels at astounding speed across the lake or simply lounges in calm waters and feeds on fish or aquatic weeds. Descriptions of the creature's size vary from 15 to 30 metres. Sometimes it has fins and sometimes feet.

The first clear sighting of Ogopogo was reported in 1926 by people parked in cars alongside the lake who all described having seen the same thing. That same year, the editor of the *Vancouver Sun* wrote: "Too many reputable people have seen [the monster] to ignore the seriousness of actual facts."

On July 2, 1947, several people in boats claimed to have seen the monster at the same time. Many contended the creature was about nine metres in length.

During the years since then, many reputable members of society, including a priest, a sea captain, a surgeon and police officers, have all claimed to have witnessed the antics of a sea monster in the lake.

Videos have been made that show something swimming in the waters of the lake. In 1968, Art Folden's film, which was taken from a hill above the shoreline, showed a dark object propelling itself through shallow water near the shore. When the film was enhanced, it clearly depicted a "reptilian-like" object.

In 1989, a used-car salesman named Ken Chaplin, together with his father Clem, claimed to have seen Ogopogo, which they described as a snake-like animal twisting, turning and flicking its tail to create a splash. People suggested that what the Chaplins saw was possibly a beaver, as tail splashing is one of its characteristics, but Ken claimed the creature he and his father saw was at least 4.5 metres long or more, which would be far too large for a beaver. Some weeks later, Ken returned with his father and daughter and filmed that same creature.

A British zoologist depicted Ogopogo as being a many-humped variety of lake monster that might in fact be a primitive serpentine whale such as the *Basilosaurus*. This theory correlates with the many sightings that claim the beast has numerous humps rather than a long neck. However, disbelievers claim the photographs and films suggest the creature is nothing more than a large otter, a beaver, or even simply a log carried along by fast-moving currents.

Whether or not one believes in the existence of Ogopogo, the lake monster has had an enormous cultural impact in the Okanagan area and beyond.

For example, in 1990, a Canadian postage stamp was issued that depicted an artist's impression of Ogopogo. In addition, in 1996, Microsoft Publisher 97 used the Ogopogo name as a mascot and codename with graphics featuring Ogopogo throughout the application's set-up program. T-shirts have also featured the monster, and in 2005 a film was made in New Zealand featuring Ogopogo. However, to ensure that no one would be offended by the filmmakers' depiction, the creature's name was changed to *Mee-Shee: The Water Giant*, and it was created in Jim Henson's Creature Shop, modelled after the late actor Walter Matthau.

Kelowna's Western Hockey League Team, the Kelowna Rockets, also features Ogopogo as their mascot, and there have been many musical releases about the monster, one of which features a track called "Ogopogo."

Numerous books, both for adults and children, telling the story of this famous monster have been written throughout the years, and the name Ogopogo has also been given to many boats and canoes.

In addition, the legend of Ogopogo has attracted a great deal of media attention, both national and international. Stories about the creature have been featured on TV shows such as *Unsolved Mysteries* and *Inside Edition,* as well as a Japanese program entitled *The World's Supernatural Phenomena.* Despite many offers of rewards for providing absolute proof of the creature's existence, no one has ever been able to claim one.

Over the years, descriptions of Ogopogo might have varied and stories might have changed with the telling, but the fact remains that something, be it real or imaginary, inhabits Okanagan Lake. Ogopogo continues to be both a mystery to the believers and pure myth to the doubters.

Today, a rather lovable-looking statue of the so-called beast can be seen on Bernard Avenue by Okanagan Lake near Kelowna's City Park.

Closer to BC's capital city, another sea monster has also caused quite a stir through the years. *Cadborosaurus willsi* (nicknamed "Caddy") is a sea serpent reported to be living in the waters of the Pacific Coast of North America. It takes its name from Cadboro Bay near Victoria and the Greek word *sauros,* meaning "lizard" or "reptile." There have been more than 300 claimed sightings of this beast during the past 200 years, many in the area of Cadboro Bay, as well as at Willis Point in the Saanich Inlet, Deep Cove near the tip of the Saanich Inlet and at Telegraph Bay near Ten Mile Point, all within a short distance of Cadboro Bay. However, Cadboro Bay claims the most sightings and has adopted Caddy as its own.

The creature is said to resemble a serpent with vertical coils or humps along its back and is alleged to have a horse-like head and long neck. Caddy's length ranges from five to 15 metres, according to witness reports.

Once again, sightings of this creature can be traced back decades to First Nations peoples' observations and tales that have spawned many legends and myths.

Ancient evidence of Caddy's existence comes from West Coast Native folklore, most especially from the Manhousat people who named the mysterious creature Hiyitl'iik, meaning "something that moves by wriggling from side to side."

There are, in fact, numerous sites along the BC coast where rock carvings or petroglyphs depict these enormous serpents, and each Native group of those early peoples had their own particular name for the creature that they claimed was often too difficult to actually describe.

But it was not until the 1930s that a *Victoria Daily Times* headline captured the world's interest announcing, "Yachtsmen tell of Huge Sea Serpent off Victoria." After that, Archie Willis, a local resident and newspaper editor, kept the public's interest in Caddy by writing about the serpent in the local media on many occasions. This prompted more people to come forward with their own stories and reports of similar sightings in the waters off Vancouver Island and, in particular, Cadboro Bay. Caddy had found a ready audience at last. After more than 1000 years of sightings from Alaska to Oregon, Caddy and his like were finally being acknowledged as a possible reality.

Sixty years later, in the 1990s, Paul H. LeBlond, a professor emeritus and retired University of British Columbia oceanographer, and Dr. Edward Bousfield, a retired Victoria-based marine biologist, gave even more credence to Caddy's existence by publishing a paper formally describing the creature as a new species. They officially named the serpent *Cadborosaurus willsi* and described it as a large aquatic reptile, 15 to 20 metres long, with a serpentine body containing a series of humps or loops when swimming near the surface, a long neck, a horse-like head and two pairs of flippers. LeBlond and Bousfield likened Caddy to his fellow cousins Nessie in Scotland and Ogopogo in Lake Okanagan.

LeBlond's paper contained information from July 1937 when a strong piece of evidence had been found in the stomach of a sperm whale at the Naden Harbour whaling station on the Haida Gwaii (Queen Charlotte) Islands. The specimen was described as "a creature of reptilian appearance, 10 foot 6 inches [3.2 metres] in length, with a head that bears close resemblance to a dog and with the features of a horse and the turned-down nose of a camel."

The carcass retrieved from the whale's stomach was photographed by two people from at least three different angles, and tissue samples were shipped off to the Nanaimo Biological Station. Mysteriously, the samples never reached their destination. Portions were also sent to the Royal British Columbia Museum in Victoria, where they were incorrectly dismissed as a fetal baleen whale. The remains of the mysterious carcass were subsequently lost and most probably forgotten until the 1990s when LeBlond wrote his paper.

Then in July and August of 1997, additional sightings further established the possible existence of the sea serpent. The first sighting in July was by two university students who stated they witnessed a creature swimming across Telegraph Bay about 14 metres from where they were sitting on a rock. It surfaced twice before disappearing into calm waters. Both students swore they were perfectly sober at the time of their encounter but were extremely puzzled by what they had seen.

A month later, a family of three cruising up Princess Louisa Inlet in a powerboat noticed what at first sight appeared to be a log lying on the glassy waters. However, as they grew closer, "the log split into three pieces and then disappeared in the water leaving only a mini-whirlpool behind it."

The same family witnessed a second sighting in August when, once again, the waters were calm as they were about to drop anchor near Homfroy Channel, adjacent to Desolation Sound. As they looked up, they noticed "an unusual wake going back and forth with a parallel set moving along beside it."

The mystery of Caddy's existence continues to this day as the believers persist in their endeavours to find the truth. In 1999, Dr. Bousfield found an article reprinted from the *Belleview American* that stated the missing carcass from July 1937 had spent one week in Belleview, Washington, where it was immersed in a vat of acetone and displayed to the public at the American Whaling Company. The journey and disappearance of this lost specimen is still under investigation.

In July 2011, an article in the *Victoria Times-Colonist* stated Caddy might have left the warmer waters of Cadboro Bay off Vancouver Island and headed north toward Alaska. A fisherman in Nushagak Bay had spotted a creature that closely resembled Caddy, or a possible relative, and an amateur video taken of the sighting, although not particularly clear, did show shapes in the water that resembled the famous sea serpent. Dr. Paul LeBlond agreed that it was the clearest video seen to date and, although somewhat grainy in appearance, the object was certainly not a whale, a seal or a large fish. In fact, the "shapes" might have been an entire family of the unknown creatures.

So has Caddy indeed left British Columbia waters and is now part of a family of sea serpents in Alaska? Or was this simply another hoax? Further reports of other "sightings" in the summer of 2011 in Alaska seem to prove that Caddy exists, and so the mystery has once again been stirred up in the depths of the ocean.

Wherever Caddy now lives—if indeed the creature does exist—BC continues to enjoy its notoriety as the site for the possible existence of at least two sea serpents in its waters—Caddy and Ogopogo—and the advocates continue to believe while the skeptics remain cynical.

Chapter Eighteen
Sasquatch—Man or Beast?

~

I n 1941 a woman named Jeannie Chapman told authorities she and her children had barely escaped from their home in Ruby Creek, BC, when a 7½ foot (2.2 metres) Sasquatch approached their house. Was the creature about to attack her? She decided not to wait around and find out.

This was not the first and would most certainly not be the last sighting of a mysterious half-man, half-beast creature in the province.

The Sasquatch, more commonly known as "Big Foot," is an apelike cryptid (any unknown living animal that is not currently recognized in the international zoological catalogues) said to inhabit the forests of the Pacific Northwest region of North America. Bigfoot has been described as a large, hairy, bipedal humanoid. The name Sasquatch comes from the Salish First Nations language meaning "wild man."

But this so-called "wild man" has never shown any aggressive tendencies. Quite the contrary—most reports of sightings claimed the creature seemed to be quite shy and retiring, always trying to avoid human contact. This apelike being has been reported as ranging in height from six to 10 feet (one to three metres) and weighing in excess of 500 pounds (226 kilograms). It is covered in dark brown or dark red hair and has large eyes, a pronounced brow ridge and a low-set forehead. The head is similar in appearance to that of a male gorilla.

Bigfoot has also been known to have a strong, unpleasant odour connected to it. Its enormous feet (measured by its footprints) are at least 24 inches (60 centimetres) long and eight inches (20 centimetres) wide, with five toes, like all known apes, although some tracks show feet with two to six toes. In any event, the size of the footprints gave rise to the creature's more popular name—Bigfoot. The tracks that also contained claw marks have been discounted because they were most probably the footprints of large bears. Bigfoot is also thought to be omnivorous and is mainly a nocturnal creature.

Most scientists question the existence of Bigfoot. They believe the stories are mainly a combination of folklore and misidentification. Some think it is all simply a grandiose hoax rather than an actual living creature. But not all scientists believe this to be the case. Some reputable scientists such as Jane Goodall and John Napier have expressed interest in Bigfoot and believe in its existence, although their claims have not been confirmed. Napier, who was once a director of the Smithsonian Institution's Primate Biology Program, wrote a book on the subject in 1973 called *Bigfoot: The Sasquatch and Yeti in Myth and Reality* in which he stated he was convinced that Sasquatch does exist, although he admitted the evidence is scientifically inconclusive.

So is Bigfoot real or simply an enduring legend?

Legends of a "wild man" have existed even before the creature had been given a name. The stories exist on every continent except Antarctica. In BC in particular, tales were told centuries ago about Ts'emekwes, a distinctly similar version of Bigfoot, and the creatures were thought to be nocturnal monsters. In 1847, Paul Kane wrote stories related by First Nations people about *skoocooms*—cannibalistic wild men living in the Pacific Northwest, particularly on the peak of Mount St. Helens in Washington State.

About one-third of all Bigfoot sightings are concentrated in the Pacific Northwest, primarily in Washington State and BC. In 1924 a man named Fred Beck wrote a book claiming the creatures were mystical beings from a completely different dimension and stated he had experienced psychic premonitions and visions concerning these apelike men. These sightings have continued through the years along the Pacific Coast from California to Alaska, and most stories are similar in content.

Nonetheless, both the scientists and the Bigfoot believers agree that many of the sightings could be hoaxes or are simply misidentified animals in the forests. Possibly as many as 70 to 80 percent of the sightings cannot be explained. Author Jerome Clark stated that the "Jacko Affair," which involved an 1884 newspaper report of an apelike creature captured in BC, was certainly a hoax. Clark claimed many newspapers at that time had regarded the alleged capture as dubious, and the *Mainland Guardian of New Westminster, British Columbia* stated categorically that "absurdity is written on the face of it."

But what is one to make of the stories and sightings that are unexplainable? Might some of them be true? In particular, the Greater Vancouver and upper Fraser Valley areas have a long history of Bigfoot sightings that date back to the 1800s—even longer if you include the ancient Aboriginal Sasquatch legends.

Possibly the earliest white-man encounter with Bigfoot in western Canada was made by the Northwest Company explorer David Thompson, who noted in his diary that during 1811, he found large footprints in the snow around the Jasper area on the British Columbia–Alberta border that were completely foreign and unexplainable.

Many reports of sightings in the Greater Vancouver area have come from the shores of Pitt Lake, the Upper Pitt River Valley, the Harrison Lake area, the Slave Lake area, Chehalis, Port Douglas, the Hemlock Valley, the Chilliwack area, Sardis, Yale, Ruby Creek and Hope. Can they all be wrong?

The skeptics, however, ask how we could share this planet with such huge creatures for generations while these beings have remained hidden for the most part, despite the many extensive searches that have been undertaken?

Nonetheless, the reported sightings continue, particularly in the Pacific Northwest. Some witnesses have described groups of these apelike creatures foraging for berries and walking upright on two legs, sometimes swimming, "whistling," screaming and verbalizing with one another.

In March 2007, two brothers reported seeing a mythical apelike creature near Tofino in July 2006 on the west coast of Vancouver Island.

"My brother and I had a strange encounter with a large, dark humanoid in the forests of Tofino," one of the men stated in the introduction to a video posted on YouTube. At the time of this writing, the video, titled "Strange Humanoid Encounter," has been viewed more than one million times.

The two brothers, who live five hours by car from Tofino, were walking in the forest and capturing wildlife footage. What they suddenly saw caught them completely off guard and rendered them temporarily speechless.

In the video, one young man finally says, "Look!... Quick!...Stay back!"

At first they assumed the creature was a bear, but the animal was at least 7 feet (2 metres) tall and was hunched over. It just stared at the two men, and by the time the two brothers got their camera up and running again, the creature had started to flee. It made absolutely no sound as it began heading through the bush. After the creature had disappeared, the men ran to where it had been standing to look for footprints, which seemed more human than bearlike.

The video is blurry and the camera work shaky, but there certainly appears to be something that looks human-like, especially when it rears up to its full height. It is when the creature is crouched over that it appears more bearlike.

Needless to say, the video provoked a great deal of discussion between the believers and the cynics. Some people believe it was a hoax while others are convinced it was the real thing.

Wildlife biologist Dr. John Bindernagel claims that numerous Sasquatch sightings are posted on YouTube every year and many appear to be hoaxes. This particular one "could well have been a Sasquatch, but it is neither persuasive nor convincing," he added.

Bindernagel states that although these Internet videos go a long way to helping scientific research into the Sasquatch, they can also be deceptive and can hinder genuine efforts to get to the truth. Nonetheless, he is convinced the Sasquatch does exist.

Reports of sightings continue in BC and throughout North America and new videos are constantly posted on YouTube. One in 2008 even claimed the body of a dead Sasquatch had been discovered in a forest in northern Georgia. After much interest from major TV networks such as the BBC, CNN, ABC News and Fox News, the two men who had posted the video admitted it was a hoax—and so yet another false report was disclosed.

There is, however, a website that frequently reports stories of people's encounters with this strange man/beast in the Pacific Northwest, and some of these reports make hair-raising tales, questioning our ability to judge whether or not we are merely being gullible. Perhaps we want to believe the stories rather than accept them as just fantasy. Is it simply wishful thinking on the part of people who would like to think we share this planet with other creatures who are like ourselves and yet so different? And are these sightings simply good publicity, enticing tourists to our province who want to try to become the one person who will discover the real truth in the wilderness of the province?

Certainly most of the scientific data that has been assembled so far provides no positive evidence to support the survival of such a large, pre-historic apelike creature throughout time. It is believed that to preserve a breeding population of such creatures, it would have been necessary for much larger numbers to have been seen to date, and that has not been the case.

Cryptozoologists explain Bigfoot as merely an unknown species of ape. The believers claiming to have seen Bigfoot think otherwise. They attribute this creature to being a phenomenon of paranormal origin.

Jeannie Chapman, the woman in Ruby Creek who reported her sighting back in 1941, was more than convinced she and her children had had an encounter with Sasquatch on that day. And no amount of scientific evidence would have persuaded her otherwise.

Chapter Nineteen

Is There a UFO Triangle in BC?

~

Sightings of unidentified flying objects (UFOs) have been reported for centuries, but most of the modern-day sightings have occurred since World War II. Certainly BC has seen its fair share of these unknown objects in the sky.

Many UFO sightings in the past 60 years have been investigated by experts from a strictly military perspective. UFO researchers have written about these events in detailed reports and even created organizations specifically devoted to the subject.

Government studies have established that most UFO sightings are probably genuine but suggest they could have been a conventional object of some kind, such as an unusual aircraft, an astronomical mass like a meteor or a bright planet, a balloon or even a strange cloud formation. A small percentage of these reported UFOs were found to be elaborate hoaxes.

However, it is also claimed that between five percent and 20 percent of the total reports are still unexplained mysteries. Many trained professionals, such as pilots, police officers and military personnel have reported seeing these objects themselves but were unable to explain them. Could they have been alien spacecraft occupied by extraterrestrial beings?

In 2007, two men in Chilliwack maintained they had seen a UFO, which one man described as "something moving from place to place as a unit and then just fading into nothing. I know I saw something that wasn't from around here because I've never seen anything move that way. It wasn't a group of birds and as it approached it broke apart into 20 or more of these little spheres...birds don't dive bomb each other like that."

Earlier, in 1969, three unrelated witnesses in Prince George saw "a strange, round object in the late afternoon sky on January 1. The sphere radiated a yellow-orange light and appeared to ascend from 2000 to 10,000 feet."

Are these reports fanciful or is there some basis of truth in them?

By far the most unusual tales of UFOs in the entire province have occurred in the north around the areas of Houston, Smithers and Terrace. In fact, so many sightings have been reported in this "triangle" that a Houston ufologist has called the area the UFO capital of Canada.

The first such sighting in this area occurred on July 29, 2002, at 10:20 PM. A Canfor employee in Houston was working late on his forklift when he saw a phosphorescent-like white ball of light with yellow undertones. It appeared to hover as it crawled across the skyline. The man called to his fellow workers.

"I called them over because I wanted to prove that I saw something and that I wasn't crazy!" he said.

The strange object grew a tail and then gained considerable speed as it headed toward Tweedsmuir Park before shooting out of sight. The entire incident had taken place in approximately 20 seconds.

The Canfor employee thought it might have been a meteorite but said "it was like no meteorite I had ever seen before. I'd seen meteor showers before, but they never looked anything like this. I really don't know what it was."

Some 20 minutes later on that same night, a teacher from nearby Quick saw a white ball of light travelling silently across the sky in a southwesterly direction, from Quick to Telkwa. Her son also saw the object.

Five minutes later, a farmer had just sat down to watch a movie after a hard day of work on his Telkwa farm. His bay window, opposite his chair, overlooked the valley below. Suddenly, a bright light flashed across the sky. Its peculiar appearance and speed amazed him. He walked outside to follow its progress, but the object had already disappeared, leaving silence in its wake.

The farmer estimated the speed of the object to be at least 650 miles (1046 kilometres) per hour and appeared to be the size of a pickup truck. "But," he added, "if you had blinked, you would have missed it."

He was so disturbed by what he saw that he woke his wife to share the experience with her. She believed him because, a few months earlier, she also had seen the same bright object travelling in the same direction. She admitted she had not told her husband at the time for fear he would think she was imagining things.

The couple were so convinced they had seen something of a paranormal nature that they telephoned the RCMP. They were told that no air force activity had been recorded in the area that night. Central Mountain Air admitted, however, that one training flight had been in the air between 10:07 and 11:04 PM, but the company's spokesperson saw no possible connection between the flight and the occurrences the couple witnessed because the Cessna 185 had a completely different flight path. In addition, the small plane would not have emitted a bright light and its engines would definitely have been heard whereas the unexplained object in the sky that night was completely silent.

Apparently a comet had also been spotted that same night, but its glowing green light and arc-shaped flight in the Hudson Bay Mountain area did not equate with these other sightings.

The reported sightings of the teacher and the farmer shared many similar features. The size, brightness, white-yellow hues of light and the speed and silence of the object were all comparable, although the teacher described the object as being an elongated circle shape, whereas the farmer said the object was definitely round in appearance. Both witnesses, however, agreed that they had definitely seen something out of the ordinary.

Two years later, in 2004, a few other unexplained UFO sightings took place in the same approximate area in BC. The first occurred at 11:20 PM on April 8 and was seen by two different residents of Smithers. Before going to bed one night, a retired teacher was giving her dog some biscuits in its dog-house on the outside deck. As she turned around to go back into the house, she saw a large, pink spherical object in the sky. It was hovering at the level of a nearby ski hill on Hudson's Bay Mountain. The object then moved toward the town, travelling down the valley. Finally, it just disappeared. The sighting lasted a few seconds, and the object made absolutely no sound. "But it did have a dark blue aura around the pink and it wasn't moving like a plane or any object I could identify. I was fasci-nated by it—and I knew I wasn't losing my marbles!"

Eight days later, on April 16 at 10:45 PM, another woman in the area saw something quite similar. She described it as a "big pink light." Her report was made without any knowledge of the first sighting. This woman worked as a homecare worker at Bulkley Lodge and was on her way to work the graveyard shift when she saw the object in the sky. "It was coming towards me, but then it backed up and disappeared," she said. She believes she was only a few blocks away from the apparition, and it was approximately "three tree lengths" above her up in the sky. It was, she said, "about the size of the full moon." Again the object made no sound, and the pink light had no distinguishing features.

On August 11 of that same year, at approximately 2:45 AM, a man was having trouble sleeping so he headed for the kitchen for a glass of water. That was when he noticed a strange light through his kitchen window. He didn't think it looked like the moon. "It was completely different and was kind of startling," he said. "It seemed to be standing in behind the trees but then it came right through the trees so you couldn't see any of the trees because of the brightness of the light. It wasn't very high in the sky but was more towards the horizon level."

On Wednesday, September 22, 2004, at 6:40 AM, a Telkwa resident on her way to work witnessed a bright yellow-white light as she travelled along the Babine Lake Road. It was moving in down from the Telkwa mountain range. She claimed the light crossed Highway 16 about 100 metres ahead of her at an altitude of approximately two or three telephone pole lengths.

The object appeared to be round in shape and glowed light green underneath. She thought it was about to crash, but it suddenly rose up again and disappeared from view. It made no sound and left no trail. Her sighting lasted approximately 15 to 20 seconds, and two other vehicles behind her must have also seen the light.

Was this a flying saucer of some kind? Was the area being visited by aliens that, at the last moment, decided not to land?

Most of these sightings were reported by sane, ordinary folk not given to illusion or imaginary visions. So what is the truth? Is there a kind of "Bermuda Triangle" in the Houston, Smithers and Terrace areas? Is the triangle of UFOs being manned by unknown beings ready to land and snap up humans? It would seem that all those bright blue, pink, green or yellow lights emanating from objects of various shapes tend to relate to science fiction of the most creative kind.

Nonetheless, Houston and Terrace have had the third and fourth highest number of UFO sightings in Canada. In 2003, Houston's 33 reported sightings were only one less than Toronto and just eight behind Vancouver, which remains the leading city for UFO sightings in Canada.

We know for sure that unexplained aerial apparitions have been seen throughout history. Even as far back as 1088 documentation can be found from a Chinese government scholar-official who wrote in his *Dream Pool Essays* about an unidentified flying object. He recorded many testimonies of eyewitnesses stating that "a flying object with opening doors would shine a blinding light from its interior that would cast shadows from trees for 10 miles [16 kilometres] in radius, and was able to take off at tremendous speeds."

In the 1800s and 1900s, reports were made of flying objects resembling a balloon flying at incredible speeds. Some appeared to be similar to a saucer in shape. *The Dennison Daily News* in 1878 was the first newspaper to coin the phrase "flying saucer."

The first post–World War II UFO sighting was claimed by an American businessman named Kenneth Arnold, who on June 24, 1947, maintained that while flying his private plane near Mount Rainier, Washington, he saw nine extremely bright objects flying across the face of Rainier. He described them as "flat like a pie pan, shaped like saucers and were so thin I could barely see them…half-moon shaped, oval in front and convex in the rear…they looked like a big flat disk or saucer."

Following that sighting, the term "flying saucer," perhaps containing extraterrestrial beings, was officially coined.

Scientific studies and government investigations continue to this day. Results are inconclusive. Experts maintain that hoaxes are not usually common because most people have absolutely no reason to claim they have seen a strange, alien object, unless they really have seen something. Therefore, some of the UFO sightings are real but simply defy explanation.

The general consensus of opinion concerning UFOs seems to be that a number of scientists do support the extraterrestrial hypothesis. Nonetheless, few scientific papers on this subject have been published. There has even been debate in the scientific community as to whether any scientific investigation into UFO sightings is warranted.

Stranger still is the fact that, for some unknown reason, much of this UFO activity has taken place in the Smithers, Houston and Terrace areas, which leads one to believe that perhaps the answer might lie in that "triangle" in northern BC.

Does northern BC in fact hold the key to a centuries-old mystery? Are we surrounded by aliens from another planet waiting to land on Earth, and have they already selected our province as their location of choice? Only time will tell.

Chapter Twenty

Vancouver Island Hauntings

~

I n 1945, two Royal Canadian Air Force pilots stayed overnight as guests at a heritage house in Oak Bay, Victoria.
They were awoken in the middle of the night by the sound
of rattling chains and saw what they believed to be a First
Nations woman standing in the room with outstretched arms,
pleading for their help. They were so shaken by the experience
that they fled the house in terror.

Five years earlier, the owners of that same house had
awoken on Christmas morning to find all their Christmas tree
decorations and cards piled in a heap on the floor by an obviously annoyed ghostly figure in the night.

This particular house on Heron Street was once owned
by John Tod and certainly has a rich and violent past conducive
to hauntings. It competes with Helmcken House in Victoria
as being the oldest structure still standing west of the Great Lakes.

John Tod was one of five original landowners in Oak
Bay when he built the house that he called "Oak Bay House"
between 1850 and 1851. By then he had retired from his position

as chief factor with the Hudson's Bay Company and wished to live on his 400-acre property in Oak Bay. He had purchased the land for the amount of 109 British pounds sterling.

Tod was an enigma in many ways. An erratic and temperamental man, he was reported to have as many as seven wives and fathered at least 10 children. Some of his wives were First Nations women, and it was known he did not treat these women well. While working for the Hudson's Bay Company, he often dealt with the First Nations population but was described by them on occasion as "the ugliest man at Fort Kamloops," where he served as chief trader for a while. It would seem he was ugly in both appearance and disposition.

Following his death in 1882, his Oak Bay property was divided among his descendants and sold off by the late 1880s. Other families to inhabit the house included the Fullers and the Paulines. Many changes were made to the original homestead throughout the years.

It was hardly surprising that eerie and unaccountable happenings were occurring there by the 1940s when such events were first recorded. The house had obviously had a rocky start under the ownership of a cruel man. In 1952, when a new heating oil tank was installed at the house, a skeleton believed to have belonged to a First Nations woman was discovered. Could this have been one of Tod's many wives? Had he murdered her and then buried her remains?

John Tod's haunted house in Oak Bay, Victoria

Subsequent owners of the house have reported other ethereal happenings, such as a rocking chair suddenly beginning to move back and forth for no apparent reason, and the latch on the door leading to the basement lifting and dropping on its own. Cups and saucers have rattled in a dresser when there were no reports of earthquakes or other phenomena in the area at the time.

Still known as Oak Bay's most haunted house, the bad vibes and unsettling events throughout the years might all stem from a woman who was disposed of many years ago and returns on occasion to protest.

Some 112 kilometres to the north of Victoria in the town of Nanaimo (known as "The Harbour City"), another house, the famous Beban House, has also reported some rather odd goings-on over the years. Since the house stopped being a family home in the 1930s, it has had been occupied by various organizations such as a daycare centre, the RCMP and Tourism Nanaimo. During those years, many encounters with the supernatural have frequently occurred. For example, preschool children at the daycare told their teacher they had seen a new child playing with them. They described this playmate as a boy with tightly braided black hair who always played with a large, red rubber ball. The children thought he was dressed strangely in what looked like a long, white nightgown. The teacher asked the children to draw his picture, and they all produced identical sketches of what appeared to be an Asian child.

Researchers discovered that at one time a young Chinese boy, the son of one of the Bebans' servants, had died tragically in the house, and it was thought the children at the daycare centre might have been seeing the ghost of this child. The long braid down his back that the children described could have been the traditional Chinese pigtail.

Beban House was once owned by lumber baron Frank Beban who had made his fortune in the lumber industry as owner of both a coal mine and the Empire Lumber Company. His wealth enabled him to purchase 160 acres of land on which stood a small farmhouse. The farmhouse was soon replaced by a new house of grand proportions in which Frank, his wife, Hannah, their three daughters and one son lived. The cost of the house was $25,000 (a great deal of money in the 1930s) and was a striking country residence with exotic gardens. The grounds even contained a racetrack.

The family enjoyed their home for more than 20 years, but by 1952, Frank's health had deteriorated, curtailing some of his business activities. He was still able to breed and train thoroughbred horses on his property, but by then only he and his wife and their servants occupied the home. The couple's children had all grown and moved away. On the morning of August 13, 1952, Frank was found dead in his bedroom, having passed away in the night. Soon afterward, the entire Beban estate was sold to the Town of Nanaimo for $53,000 and used as a sports park with new outbuildings added to the grounds. However, the rustic old house, once an impressive landmark, soon began to deteriorate and by the 1990s was in a sad state of repair. In 1995 the town declared the house a heritage site and, with assistance from the provincial government, restoration began on the mansion so it could be used to help enhance the town of Nanaimo.

Even after the house passed from the Beban family to the Town of Nanaimo, the strange happenings have continued. Other occupants swore that in the original owner's trophy room, a cupboard door kept opening on its own, while filing cabinets in the offices kept opening for no apparent reason. Creaks and groans have often been heard on the staircase, and the tinkling of teacups mixed with the sound of women's voices are frequently heard coming from an empty room that had once been the front parlour. A loud yell broke the silence on one occasion as well as a thumping from an upstairs bedroom that was unoccupied. Lights are often seen to be burning in the house at night when it is empty. On another occasion, a woman dressed in a long, blue gown was clearly seen standing in a doorway. When the employee who saw her asked if she needed help, the apparition literally disappeared into thin air.

The voices of chattering women and the tinkling of teacups might have been from past tea parties given by Mrs. Beban, and the loud yell from upstairs might have been the ghost of Frank Beban himself calling out before he died.

The thumps and creaks, a constantly running toilet and even flying objects might be easily explained, but the staff of the various organizations occupying the house through the years cannot explain other events that have transpired. Sometimes they would find a doorknob unscrewed or a weird, unintelligible message left on the answering machine overnight. Many of these things seemed more prevalent at Halloween or Christmas and caused people to wonder why so much spiritual energy was in the house. Most of it, however, appears harmless to the witnesses who swear by what they've seen.

In view of all this activity, a psychic was invited to explore the house to explain what might be going on. She went into the boiler room in the basement but found the atmosphere there so unpleasant that she could hardly breathe. She refused to enter the house ever again.

Most of the ghostly happenings at Beban House are harmless, while others, such as finding door handles removed, are simply irritating. Is there a ghost at large?

Another house, farther up-island in the Comox Valley, is said to have a resident ghost known as "Aunt Anna." Her presence has been felt in the house since 1938, approximately 18 years after a woman of the same name died. The only people who have ever seen Aunt Anna were 12-year-old girls—one saw her in 1938 and the other in 1998, and both told the same story, giving her name and the same description of her.

This particular house, known as Sandwick Manor, was built by Eric Duncan in 1912 for his wife Anna and their adopted son Charles. Sadly, Charles was killed during World War I, and Anna, who suffered from severe arthritis, died shortly afterward. Eric decided to sell the house because it had become too big for him.

The house has always been a happy home for those who have lived there since, so Aunt Anna's visits have often simply been explained as mischievous pranks she has enjoyed playing on subsequent owners. Any paranormal activity has only involved a "misty glow" that has appeared in a spare bedroom.

On some occasions, animals in the house seem to sense Aunt Anna's presence. Two dogs, a cat and a bird will often all simultaneously stare at a spot on the ceiling—and yet there is nothing there that can be seen by the human eye.

Four other houses back in Victoria also have resident ghosts. The Point Ellice House along the Gorge waterway is situated on Pleasant Street and is now owned by the provincial government and is run as a heritage attraction. The house was owned by one family, the O'Reillys, for over 100 years, and many of the "hauntings" have been connected to members of that once well-known family in Victoria.

Today, this house is situated in a quiet oasis of beauty amid an industrial neighbourhood of downtown Victoria. Designed by architect John Teague, it was built in 1861 for Charles W. Wallace. However, from 1863 onwards, it was owned by the Peter O'Reilly family and is best known as the O'Reilly house because the family had lived there for so long.

Some 30 years after her death, the ghost of Kathleen O'Reilly, the daughter of the O'Reillys, appeared one day to conduct a tour through the house for tourists. She was dressed in a period gown of the times. During the 1960s, some Australian women camping on the grounds were awakened by the voice of an irritated woman telling them to leave her property immediately, but once they had gathered up their belongings and were about to leave, the women realized there was absolutely no one there. Could the voice have been that of Caroline O'Reilly, once the chatelaine of this home?

Tourists visiting the house in the 1970s were waiting for the then O'Reilly owner to escort them through her home when another woman in a period costume appeared before them to conduct the tour. She then disappeared, and the current owner returned. The tourists told the homeowner to "thank the lady in the blue costume" for the tour that they had much enjoyed. The owner was puzzled but intrigued by the description of the "blue costume" so she led the tourists to the bedroom of Kathleen, Caroline O'Reilly's daughter. There, on display on the bed, was the identical dress once owned by Kathleen and which the tourists claimed the "lady" had been wearing. Kathleen O'Reilly had been dead for more than three decades at that time, and her dress had been laid out on the bed for visiting tourists to view. Had Kathleen returned to her beloved home to make her final appearance that day?

It is also claimed that a light is often seen at night passing beneath the Port Ellice Bridge near the house. There appears to be no apparent source of the flashing light unless, as many believe, it is the ghost of someone searching for a loved one lost in the tragedy of 1896 when the bridge collapsed. This heritage attraction is certainly an enigma—full of magic, myth and the strong presence of a family who once dominated the area.

Experts believe there are four possible reasons for the many ghostly apparitions that have formed part of the story of this beautiful house. First, the fact that one prominent family inhabited this home for so long would make their presence strongly felt long after their demise. Second, the house is close to water that conducts the necessary energy needed for such ethereal happenings. Third, the house was once set in a peaceful and tranquil spot but is today surrounded by the noise of industry, which can be unsettling for spirits. The final reason concerns an event that occurred in 1896 when nearby Point Ellice Bridge collapsed, plunging more than 50 people to their deaths in the Gorge waterway. Any disaster such as this produces an aftermath of great electricity and emotion.

The owner of another house on Mount Douglas X Road in Victoria has often had a vision of a man in a tweed jacket appear as a reflection in a mirror while frequent swirls of mists materialize for no apparent reason.

Upon investigation of this 1912 house, owners discovered that the people living there during the 1920s and early 1930s were well-to-do folk who often entertained on a grand scale. Their visitors came from around the world, and one gentleman in particular, who came from Germany, fell in love with the young lady of the house. His feelings, however, were not reciprocated and she rejected his attentions. In utter despair, one night he apparently hanged himself in the attic. Does this

German gentleman revisit the house to this day, anxiously searching for his lost love?

Another theory about this particular house that stands on an incongruous bend in an otherwise straight road, is that the house was originally built directly over a First Nations burial path. Could this explain or account for the many ghostly encounters throughout the years?

Yet another house near Ten Mile Point is full of enchanting myths, legends and a resident ghost, but it also has one closet that seems to contain a ghostly presence. This mystical house was built in 1912 and has had an eclectic and eerie past, starting with the strange disappearance of the original owner. The gentleman had built the original structure to be used as a large ballroom (which over the years has been added onto and expanded upon). He had it built for his daughter to host parties for her friends.

One day, he took off in his rowboat into the nearby bay and was never seen again. The building was abandoned and later was supposed to become an orphanage for English children set to sail to Canada during World War I. However, between February and September 1915 when the children were set to sail, some 50 ships, including the ill-fated *Lusitania,* were hit by German submarines. It was assumed the children were either lost at sea, or else never left England due to the inherent danger on the high seas.

The "ballroom" then became a hospital for wounded veterans and more bedrooms were added on the upper level.

Many more colourful stories have been told about subsequent owners, some fact and some fiction. For example, it was rumoured the house was once a gambling den with liquor being brought in from nearby Smugglers' Cove. Following World War II, the building was again a hospital. A shooting was said to have occurred in the ballroom. Another patient reportedly had his leg amputated in the ballroom.

One wonders whether the subsequent hauntings experienced by the current owner are simply a part of that colourful scenario from the past—the odd disappearance of the original owner, the lost orphans, smuggled liquor and gambling, a shooting and an agonizing operation. The current owner, who is a teacher, writer, printmaker, storyteller and illustrator of children's books, would like to think so. It all adds to the myths and magic of her home today.

Owners of a fourth house in the capital city are convinced of ghostly visitors—a man smoking a pipe and a small woman in white with arms outstretched. Guests at the house, which was run as a bed and breakfast for many years, had often related similar experiences and eerie feelings.

The house was once owned by a Captain Walker, an English sea-faring man of note who travelled the world. While in Japan, he met and married a beautiful Japanese woman, Sato Fukada, who bore him nine children. After leaving Japan, they briefly returned to England where Sato died of heart disease at the age of 36. Today she lies buried in Cumberland.

Eventually, the broken-hearted captain left England and came to Canada, acquiring land on Vancouver Island. In 1915 he built the home that today some claim is haunted by him and his wife. The current owners believe Sato is upset because she was buried in England, far away from where her husband and family are now buried in Canada. Periodically she visits the house, which she was never able to see in her lifetime.

If Victoria is the most haunted city in British Columbia, one of the most haunted spots in the heart of the capital city itself is definitely Bastion Square. The square is part of the old town section, which is full of interesting alleys and courtyards that are conducive to hauntings and paranormal experiences.

The most prominent building in the square was once the old Police Barracks. Many criminals were held at the barracks before they were hanged in the square. The jail yard was said to be the scene of at least 11 public hangings during the 1860s and 1870s. After the hanging had taken place, if no loved one came forward to claim their dead relative or friend, the body was buried beneath the yard in a pit of quicklime. No markers were placed on these primitive graves, so perhaps these poor souls, most often hung for relatively minor offences, are the ones who return to haunt the square today.

Sir Matthew Baillie Begbie, a well-known judge in early BC history dubbed "the hanging judge," was supposedly the one responsible for condemning many countless of these criminals to "hang by the neck until dead" in the days of the early frontier. History, however, proves otherwise as he apparently heard only 52 cases as a Supreme Court Judge during his career and sentenced only 27 of those men to death. That is a surprisingly low number considering the wild, lawlessness of those days of shootings and murders.

In 1965, having served briefly as a temporary City Hall, the old Police Barracks building was converted into what is now the Maritime Museum. It is said that Judge Begbie's "presence'" is still part of the building to this day. Staff in the museum claim to have experienced numerous hauntings by the old judge.

Certainly Bastion Square is definitely a place of high energy—and this was the case long before the coming of the white man in 1843. First Nations people, whose population numbered in the thousands, dwelt on this site before a smallpox epidemic overtook them, which had them scattering farther afield. Historian and writer John Adams relates stories during his "Haunted Walking Tours" through the city of a sacred rock known as Pal-at-sis, which sits across the harbour from Bastion Square at Songhees Point. The rock had magical powers and is talked about in many First Nation legends. It was supposedly sought by mothers wishing to protect their children from disease. Men were said to gain strength from simply touching the legendary rock.

These kind of supernatural stories have served to increase the ghostly tales surrounding Bastion Square down through the years. For instance, at Number 19 Bastion Square, a phantom organist can be heard playing his organ at night when everything is quiet. There are also so-called phantoms heard in nearby Helmcken Alley on the south side of the square. The alley was named for the once-famous fort doctor, John Sebastian Helmcken, whose office was in a small log building on that site.

His actual home still stands today a few blocks away from where his surgery once stood in Helmcken Alley. Both Helmcken House and Helmcken Alley claim paranormal properties. The house is often said to be "occupied" by the old doctor or his youngest daughter, and people walking by the alley frequently tell nearby shopkeepers that they hear the clanking of heavy chains and footsteps sounding like heavy boots marching in the narrow passageway. As this was also the same path traditionally used by chain gangs in early Victoria, it begs the question whether those early chained prisoners have returned to haunt their old stomping ground.

Burnes House at Number 516 Bastion Square also contains stories of hauntings. The building is named after Tommy Burnes, an Irish entrepreneur during the Fraser River Gold Rush days. He was well known in Victoria in those early years as a hotel and saloon owner. By 1888 he had also opened the "Burnes House" hostelry, which catered to members of the legal profession and other travellers. A few years later, rumour has it that Burnes House had fallen into decline and had become a brothel. Perhaps because of this unfounded rumour, the ghosts that have been seen in this building are mostly women whose appearance is similar to ladies of ill repute. Over the years, Burnes House has been converted into a warehouse, some boutique shops, offices and even a language college. Various sightings have been reported during this time, but most are of women floating through the rooms in a ghostly fashion. Could these be the ladies of the night from a different era?

Numerous other apparitions are said to visit the many buildings of Bastion Square today. Most can be accounted for because of the colourful past that once existed on this site in Victoria. But can all these strange hauntings be explained away?

Vancouver Island in general and Victoria in particular seem to have their fair share of ghostly happenings, and one can only speculate the reason for them. Are they all figments of over-active imaginations? Or are they real?

In his book *Ghosts and Legends of Bastion Square,* Adams points out that Victoria "has the distinction of being the most haunted city in British Columbia and the Pacific Northwest." He also adds, however, that "a ghost story…is first and foremost *just* a *story* and preferably should be a story well told."

Could there be some special extra energy at work in Victoria and throughout Vancouver Island because, as some suggest, of the long period of human occupation there?

Two Haunted Houses in Agassiz?

In one private residence in Agassiz there is said to be "jokester" at large. A ghost who likes to play tricks on its residents has been nicknamed "Charlie." Charlie comes and goes at will and delights in moving items around the house.

Another Agassiz house had a more troublesome ghost that would often open the front door and leave it open when no one was home. This lady ghost had also been seen in a window, appearing to be putting a record on an old-fashioned record player. Many occupants of this house in the past had experienced illness, one of whom had died.

As the ghost was being rather a nuisance, the current owner decided to have a "letting go" party at which she and her neighbours held hands and prayed for the "dear departed lady," asking her to please leave the house immediately. They claimed to have seen a light moving slowly across the wall for about 20 minutes. It became smaller and smaller until it was just a pinpoint. Then it disappeared completely. The hauntings ended from that night onwards.

First Nations people were known to live there from the late 1700s, and evidence has been found to confirm human existence even long before that. Other people believe the rock formation underneath the island could account for the extra forces of energy at work that are conducive to these ethereal happenings.

People who enjoy the ghostly stories hardly seem to care about the reasons or explanations for the sightings. They simply choose to believe.

Chapter Twenty-one
The Cariboo Camels

~

One day back in the early 1860s, a First Nations man known as Tanas Johnny was digging postholes along the border line of Robert Scott's property in the area of Gordon Head when he saw an apparition.

Robert Scott was one of the 13 original landowners near Mount Douglas, on the southern tip of Vancouver Island. Scott's property bordered that of James Tod at the base of the mountain, and Tanas Johnny was one of many Native people who worked for Tod.

Tanas Johnny was an honest man. He was also a hard worker and, on the day in question, was methodically digging for clams at Mount Douglas beach before making more postholes along the pasture border of his boss' property.

Johnny had long believed in the legends and mystique of the land—legends such as the great Sea-Bear and the Woman of the Woods known as Dosonoqua. He had witnessed lightning leap from the eyes of a Thunderbird and he had heard the thunder of the bird's wings as it lifted its prey from the water. These legends were ingrained in his soul and he knew them to be true.

But as he knelt to scoop water from a posthole he had dug the day before, the small man was suddenly engulfed in great fear because of something completely unknown to him. At first he smelled something strange, and then he saw an eerie shadow looming up behind him. He turned in panic, convinced he was being confronted by some kind of devil-snake or sea-devil.

Before him stood a creature that was completely foreign to him. The creature had two humps and stood all of seven feet (two metres) high. He imagined it must weigh nearly a tonne, and to Tanas Johnny it was the devil on the loose. Nothing would have convinced him otherwise. Terrified, he dropped his tools and ran until he reached the safety of his shack, but he knew that it was already too late. For him this was the end. He was convinced he would die because he had seen what he perceived to be the devil. Legend had it that once a man had seen the devil, he would die soon afterward. In keeping with those beliefs, the strength slowly left his body and he passed away.

What Tanas Johnny had seen, and what had most probably caused him to have a heart attack, was simply a camel. But he would not have known there was such a creature; in fact, there was no word for "camel" in the Chinook language at that time.

More importantly, Johnny did not know that about two dozen camels had recently been imported into BC from California by three gentlemen—Adam Heffley, Henry Ingram and Frank Laumeister—for use as pack animals in the Cariboo.

But how could one of the camels have appeared in the region of Mount Douglas? And, if not a camel, what did poor Tanas Johnny really see?

The saga of the Cariboo camels dates back to March 1, 1862, when an advertisement appeared in the *Colonist* offering camels for sale by a San Francisco merchant who had purchased them from the U.S. Army Camel Corps, where they had successfully been used to carry heavy freight. The ad said the camels had worked in Arizona on railway construction and had also been used as pack animals during the California Gold Rush.

It was hoped the camels could be used to freight goods along the Old Cariboo Road from Lillooet to Alexandria and would be a great addition in the Cariboo area. The advertisement had attracted the attention of a Lillooet man named John Calbreath who purchased 23 of these animals at $300 a head, acting on instructions from Heffley, Ingram and Laumeister. It was Frank Laumeister's name, however, that eventually became associated with the camel venture.

The camels arrived on April 15, 1862, on the steamship *Hermann*. During their brief stay in Victoria, the animals garnered much interest from the city's citizens, especially when one camel delivered a baby and another escaped from the pack and was not seen again until the fall.

Sketch of a two-humped camel. John Calbreath of Lillooet, BC, purchased 23 of these camels in 1862.

~

The rest were loaded onto a barge in May and towed by the *Flying Dutchman* to New Westminster. By the middle of the month they were already at work on Pemberton Road.

In the beginning, everything seemed to be going well. The creatures could carry up to 600 pounds (270 kilograms), twice as much as the mules, and were good foragers. Their feet were their main drawback—they were suited to sand and easily torn to shreds by the rough terrain of the Cariboo countryside. Apparently, canvas boots were made for them in an attempt to solve this problem. By the end of June, the first camels had left Lillooet for Alexandria, and soon after a newspaper reported that one camel died when it slid off a cliff.

More reports began drifting back to Victoria, and most were far from encouraging. Stagecoach drivers and miners alike were complaining bitterly about the camels, saying their horses were terrified of them and would bolt whenever they encountered a camel on the road. In addition, the camels were eating anything and everything they could find—pants, shirts, hats and bars of soap were fast disappearing from campsites. Even Sir Mathew Baillie Begbie, the famous Cariboo judge, developed a hatred for the beasts when one of them caused his horse to bolt, leaving him clinging to his saddle for dear life.

The camels, stubborn by nature, had other disparaging habits such as a tendency to spit at the slightest provocation. Furthermore, their odour was both offensive and, because it was unfamiliar, was feared by everyone that came into contact with them. At least a dozen of the beasts appear to have survived their first season in the Cariboo and were said to have wintered at Quesnel Forks.

By the following May, the camels were back at work in Lillooet, but their owners were once again the subject of lawsuits and threats of legal action. Miners and stagecoach owners were becoming increasingly annoyed by the camels' appearance on the trails, which caused their horses to stampede.

Frank Laumeister finally decided to dispose of his camels for good. Some of the beasts were taken over by local ranchers, either as pets or as working animals. One was shot when it was mistaken for a grizzly bear. That particular camel, shot by miner John Morris, ended up on the menu at a hotel near Beaver Lake.

For many years afterwards, camel sightings continued throughout the Cariboo. The last known surviving camel, known as Lady, lived on a ranch in Westwold, BC, which in those days was known as Grande Prairie, and it died sometime between 1896 and 1905. The camel had simply leaned against a tree and died on its feet.

So what happened to Frank Laumeister, who by 1868 was the principle owner of the Cariboo camels? One report stated he drowned in San Francisco Bay in 1878, but he actually died in Arizona in 1891 and was buried in Tucson. His daughter, Pauline, married famous stagecoach driver Stephen Tingley, who was known for driving at high speeds along the narrow Cariboo Trail. Unlike other stagecoach drivers, he obviously did not harbour any hostility toward his father-in-law because of the camels.

Today, two areas in the Cariboo commemorate the 1860s camel experiment that went so wrong. One is Camelsfoot Range and the other is the Bridge of the 23 Camels in Lillooet. And there is some suggestion that the ghosts of these strange beasts of burden still haunt part of the Cariboo to this day.

But what of poor Tanas Johnny who died of a heart attack in his shack on southern Vancouver Island as a result of the "vision" he had seen, a vision that he believed to be the devil himself? What really happened? Did he in fact see the one camel that supposedly escaped from the camel train on arrival in Victoria in 1862? A First Nations legend would have us believe otherwise.

Chapter Twenty-two

Some Provincial Folklore

~

There are numerous folklore stories throughout the province, and the British Columbia Folklore Society has collected many of these unusual tales. This organization delights in hearing local legends and is always looking for more. This chapter provides a sample of some of those legendary tales.

Take, for example, the story of how the popular Forbidden Plateau area near Campbell River on Vancouver Island came by its name. The plateau, which is situated on the lower slopes of Mount Becher, is well known today as a recreational area for skiing, hiking, biking and climbing, but according to the Comox First Nations people, there is another, much darker side to the area that explains how it came to be called Forbidden.

At one time, slavery and capture was common among all the coastal tribes and occurred when enemies attacked one another from the sea in their canoes. The Comox Nation was often threatened, so they decided to send all their women and children to a higher plateau for safety. On one occasion while under attack from the nearby Cowichan First Nations, all the women and children simply disappeared. Since then, it is "forbidden" to go to the plateau because it is believed to be inhabited by evil spirits that once devoured all those who ventured there.

~

Another place of legend is Cultus Lake in the Fraser Valley. The Chilliwack First Nations call Cultus Lake "Swehl-tcha," which refers to the time when it was supposedly nothing but an empty basin. The word "cultus" is derived from early Chinook jargon used by the traders in the Northwest, meaning "worthless" or "bad," especially when used as an adjective attached to a person's name. And when placed together with the word "potlatch" (a ceremony of gift giving), it took on the meaning of "a gift of little or no value."

The legend of Cultus Lake, however, describes the fact that the First Nations people believed the lake was bottomless. But at one time, before it was even a lake, the area contained several small creeks that disappeared into an underground passage where Cultus Lake is today. There is a story of a young man who went swimming in one of those creeks and was suddenly swept away by a strong current.

Much later, some distance away at Mud Bay between White Rock and Point Roberts, a group of young men who were spearing seals discovered a body. The body was identified as that of the man who had gone swimming and had disappeared, apparently through an underground river that came to the surface at Mud Bay.

Chilliwack First Nations legends also report the existence of a three-foot-long (91-centimetre) devilfish and a 14-inch (35-centimetre) blackfish. Both are saltwater fish but were found on the beach of Cultus Lake. How would the fish have got there from the ocean? These odd occurrences, including the apparent appearance of supernatural monsters, have all defined the name given to Cultus Lake—a worthless or bad place.

~

Today, the town of Fernie in the Elk Valley of the East Kootenays in southeastern BC is a prosperous community situated in a tranquil and beautiful setting. It could also be subject to a curse placed on an old prospector back in 1887. The prospector was William Fernie, the founder of the town, who once broke a promise made to a First Nations chief. William had noticed the chief's daughter was wearing a necklace of shining black stones that William knew to be coal. He asked the chief where the stones could be found, and the chief promised to show him if William promised to marry his daughter.

After being shown the location of the coal deposits, William refused to follow through on his promise. The chief was so angered by the white man's broken word that he placed a curse on the entire valley. From that day forward, he said the valley would suffer from fire, flood and famine.

Since then, Fernie has experienced a series of disasters and tragedies that other nearby regions have escaped. The city has had mine explosions, one of which killed at least 128 men. In 1904, a massive fire burned down much of the town's business section. Four years later, in 1908, a forest fire nearly destroyed the entire city, leaving only 32 buildings standing and almost all 6000 residents homeless. In 1916, the Elk River overflowed its banks and flooded large sections of West Fernie. Near-famine conditions occurred during the Great Depression, causing Fernie residents to firmly believe there must be some truth to the old curse. They wondered if it would ever be over.

Were these disasters mere coincidences? Perhaps, but many claim that on summer evenings, a ghostly shadow in the form of a First Nations princess sitting astride her horse with her father standing alongside is visible on a rock-face high above the town. The pair appears to gaze down on the valley the chief had cursed so long ago.

In any event, in August 1964, members of the Kootenay tribe, led by Chief Red Eagle, gathered in Fernie for a ceremony to lift the "Fernie Curse." Fernie's mayor smoked the "pipe of peace" with Chief Red Eagle and apologized for William

Fernie's broken promise in 1887. Life has since been a little more peaceful in Fernie.

~

Yet another Fernie legend is that of "Griz," which tells of a baby boy born in 1879 in the midst of a bitterly cold winter. He was supposedly born in a grizzly bear cave high in the mountains surrounding Fernie. When the hungry bear awoke from hibernating, it saw the child as a meal. A vicious battle ensued between the bear and the little boy, and the noise of their fight woke the people of Fernie. The next morning, the townsfolk set off for the mountain, looking everywhere to see what had caused such a disturbance. One man thought he saw a small boy wearing a bearskin and hat leaping from rock to rock. The man's friends laughed at his tale, and eventually the story was forgotten.

The area is now known as Snow Valley and is popular with skiers. Most recently, some skiers were climbing the peaks above the ski area during a heavy snowstorm. While pausing to catch their breath, they suddenly saw a curious sight. Above them stood a man of great height carrying a musket 8 feet (2.4 metres) long. They estimated the man was at least 300 pounds (136 kilograms). He was wearing a grizzly fur coat with a bearskin hat pulled down over his eyes. As the skiers watched in silence, the man began shooting the musket into the sky, making even more snow fall from above. The delighted tourists were thrilled with the extra powder.

When the skiers returned from the mountain, they told everyone of their extraordinary experience. Some old-timers nodded in agreement as they recalled the story of the boy in the grizzly-bear clothing, plus a later discovery of large, barefooted tracks on the mountain peaks.

To celebrate the resurrection of this old legend, the town held a weeklong festival with sporting events, parades and parties to honour the boy-bear who they have named Griz, their snow powder king. This festival is still held in Fernie every February, where the best powdery ski conditions continue to bless the mountains—or so the story goes.

∼

If you look up from Fernie toward Three Sisters Mountain and Proctor Mountain, you can witness another legend. Many years ago, a young First Nations chief was finding it difficult to select one of three beautiful sisters for a bride. The older chiefs asked the gods to help them force the chief to make up his mind. But the gods believed procrastination was a heinous sin and that a serious punishment should be cast upon the indecisive chief.

It was decreed the young chief should be turned into a mountain, and every day he would be forced to look at what he could never have. The three women were so saddened by this news that they prayed they also might be turned into mountains. Their prayers were answered.

Today, people who gaze upon the Three Sisters and Proctor mountains are really looking at these three women and the young chief who couldn't decide which one to choose for his bride.

These are just a few examples of the many folklore legends worth sharing in British Columbia.

Chapter Twenty-three

The Legend of Christmas Hill

~

C hristmas can bring out the very best or the very worst in people. The final story in this book, be it legend or truth, shows humanity at its best and ends this narrative on a positive note. At the same time, the story describes how a small hill a few kilometres from the centre of Victoria came by its name—Christmas Hill.

Soon after the establishment of Fort Victoria in 1843, legend has it that on Christmas Eve, a large black bird swooped down out of the darkened sky and hovered over a First Nations village alongside the fort, near to where the Parliament Buildings stand today. The bird looked down over a baby lying in its papoose basket and picked up the child in its claws before soaring off into the night sky.

The child's mother was naturally grief-stricken as she saw her baby disappearing from sight. She frantically began to call for help from her tribe members, running back and forth in a distraught state. She soon managed to rally assistance, not only from her own tribe but also from other tribes who had seen her despair. In addition, the local white fur traders from the Hudson's Bay Company and most of the nearby settlers all gathered around, asking how they could help.

A large group of men soon set off on foot with the mother in the direction the bird had flown. They carried flaming torches to light their way as the night grew darker. The group feared they would never find the infant but were determined to try anyway.

Men of all colours and backgrounds banded together—First Nations, English, Scottish, Irish, French, Italian and Chinese, among others—and searched the dense forest that surrounded the fort at that time. They were determined to help the woman find her lost child.

Many of those in the search party were of the Christian faith and were thinking about the birth of the Holy Child they would be celebrating the next day. The sky suddenly began to lighten somewhat and the brilliance of the stars helped light their way.

Early on Christmas morning, the missing child was finally found. The large bird had apparently placed the baby on the summit of a small hill approximately 3.5 miles (5.5 kilometres) from the fort. The baby had been covered in leaves to keep him warm. As the ecstatic and greatly relieved mother bent over her child, he smiled up at her as though trying to reassure her that he was unharmed despite his perilous adventure.

Legend has it that from that night onwards, the small hill became known as Christmas Hill. The name is mentioned on the earliest surveyors' maps of the area. Sadly, the legend was forgotten over time, and eventually the hill's name was changed to the more ordinary Lake Hill, which was also the name of that immediate area.

In 1937, the Montague Bridgman family built a house on the summit of the hill and decided to resurrect the old legend by calling their home Christmas Hill. Since then, the legend has been recognized, and the hill's name has been acknowledged as Christmas Hill once again.

Little Christmas Hill is 15 metres lower than nearby Mount Tolmie, named for an earlier premier, Simon Fraser Tolmie, and is less than half the height of Victoria's other little mountain, Mount Douglas, named for the father of British Columbia himself, Sir James Douglas. But its presence is significant in Greater Victoria.

Christmas Hill rises above land once occupied by the old Mackenzie Farm, owned by an early settler, Kenneth MacKenzie, who arrived in the area in the 1850s to act as a farm bailiff for the Pacific Agricultural Society, a subsidiary of the Hudson's Bay Company.

Today, from the summit of Christmas Hill, you can look down on magical Swan Lake, and in the opposite direction,

Lost Lake, so named when a naval officer visiting the area in the 1850s went out on a hunting expedition and became lost until he was safely found by other hunters and brought back to the fort.

And despite being so close to BC's capital city, Christmas Hill has managed to retain an aura of rural beauty and has become a nature lover's haven and a popular gathering place for botanists and bird lovers alike. Even the construction of a gated community of condominiums has not spoiled the beauty of Christmas Hill.

If legends are to be believed, it was a bird of a different ilk, raven-like in appearance, that once stole a child away from its mother and gently carried it to a site that could easily be found, thereby giving the little hill its name.

So one might question the purpose of this strange act. Why would the bird have caused a mother such pain only to allow the story to end happily? There are many theories bandied about, but perhaps the most significant one was that it was a lesson to teach humans the importance of working together in times of need, regardless of colour, creed or race.

The message that was delivered those many years ago in the mythical form of a legend is just as important today as we constantly witness the strong human spirit of caring for one another, which always seems to come to the fore as we share our hardships and adversities.

It seems that throughout time, this message has been apparent, against all odds and when times seem their darkest. Is it a legend? Or simply a message of truth?

Conclusion

~

As noted in the introduction to this book, British Columbia has always been famous for its rain forests, its rivers, its lakes, its mountains and its overall amazing beauty. The province is perhaps not so well known for its mysteries, unsolved crimes or tales of the paranormal.

The prominent murder cases that have turned cold over time, such as that of Janet Smith, Molly Justice and Lindsay Buziak, are both frustrating and baffling to the authorities who want them resolved once and for all. But answers and closure are not always forthcoming, and sometimes crimes can take years or even decades to solve.

But other mysteries, such as Hetty Fredrickson's changing painting and the sightings of Caddy and Ogopogo, are mystical in content and possibly beyond human understanding; they truly define the meaning of a mystery. Equally mysterious are the marine stories of jumbo squids, whales, a graveyard of wrecked ships and the appearance of feet on BC's beaches.

And then there are the horrors that have taken place throughout BC's history, such as the story of Agnes McVee at the Mile 108 Hotel in the Cariboo during the 1870s, which contrasts with the miracle birth that occurred against all odds at the Wigwam Inn. The McVee story might have been exaggerated and is hopefully nothing more than a legend. The Wigwam Inn story is true and was a miracle of the first degree—a wonderful and amazing event. Miracles are always good for the soul because they offer us hope, like the legend of Christmas Hill. It would be incredibly amazing if other miracles could occur in cases such as the Michael Dunahee disappearance and all the missing young women along the Highway of Tears.

There are many more unspeakable crimes and criminals who unfortunately have put BC on the map for all the wrong reasons, such as two of the most notorious serial killers in Canadian history—Clifford Olson and Robert Pickton. Both men are sadistic murderers of the worst kind.

Olson confessed in 1982 to killing 11 young men and women, one as young as nine years old, in the most horrendous and cruel manner by abducting, raping, strangling or bludgeoning his victims to death. The locations of many of his victims were not known until he somehow managed to strike a controversial deal with police who paid his family $100,000 in exchange for his help leading investigators to where he had disposed of some of the bodies. How could such an unspeakable "deal" have happened?

More recently, Robert Pickton, a pig farmer from Port Coquitlam near Vancouver, was convicted of second-degree murder for killing six women and was charged in the deaths of an additional 20. His particular targets were prostitutes and drug users from Vancouver's downtown eastside. The families of many of his other victims still don't have answers and have been unable to find any closure.

Fortunately, Pickton is now behind bars with no hope of ever being released, and Olson died in prison on September 30, 2011.

While researching all the stories I have included in this book, one fact became apparent: the tales told here are merely a fraction of the numerous mysteries, legends and unsolved crimes in BC. There are a multitude of other stories yet to be told.

Notes on Sources

Chapter 1: The Murder of Constable Johnston Cochrane

Sheldan, Constable J.P.R. "History of Fallen Heroes," Victoria City Police Archives, 2009–10.

Chapter 2: Who Killed William Robinson?

BCA Attorney General documents, GR419. Morley, J.P. Sworn testimonial of Sue Tas (Dick), April 7, 1869.

British Colonist, March 24, 1869; Editorial, April 13, 1869; June 24, 1869.

Daily British Columbian, June 3, 1869. Court of Assize Before Chief Justice Needham, June 3, 1869.

Higgins, D.W. *The Passing of a Race.* Toronto, ON: William Briggs, 1905.

www.canadianmysteries.ca/sites/robinson/home/indexen.html

Chapter 3: The Cariboo Mile 108 Hotel Murders

www.historical.bc.ca/murder.html

Chapter 4: Who was the Real Ten Mile Point Murderer?

Green, Valerie. *Upstarts and Outcasts: Victoria's Not-So-Proper Past.* Victoria, BC: Touchwood Editions, 2000.

Victoria Times-Colonist, November 1898.

Chapter 5: The Vicious Slaying of Agnes Bings

Patterson, T.W. *Murder, Brutal, Bizarre & Unsolved Mysteries of the Northwest,* Victoria, BC: Solitaire Publications, 1973.

Chapter 6: The Scottish Nightingale

Lazarus, Eve. *At Home with History: The Untold Secrets of Greater Vancouver's Heritage Homes.* Vancouver, BC: Anvil Press, 2007.

McNicoll, Susan. *British Columbia Murders: Mysteries, Crimes and Scandals.* Canmore, AB: Altitude Publishing, 2003.

Starkins, Edward. *Who Killed Janet Smith?* Toronto, ON: MacMillan of Canada, 1984.

Vancouver Sun and *Vancouver Province*, 1924, 1925.

Chapter 7: The Death of Doukhobor Leader Peter Verigin

Ewashen, Larry A. "A Brief History of Peter, The Lordly, Verigin," www.columbiariver.ca/doukhobor/Peterbook.html

Remarks by the Honourable Iona Campagnolo, PC, CN, OBC, Lieutenant-Governor of British Columbia, Royal BC Museum, Victoria, BC. April 27, 2006.

Chapter 8: No Justice for Molly

Bell, Jeff. "Judge's Report Dismisses Theories of Murder Cover-up." *Times-Colonist*, September 5, 1996.

Kines, Lindsay, and Rob Shaw. "Cold Cases: Seamstress's Killing a 65-year-old Mystery." *Victoria Times-Colonist*, October 19, 2008.

Personal interview with Inspector Rob McColl, Saanich Police Department, March 12, 2009.

Taylor, Martin R., QC. "A Review of the Conduct of the Criminal Law, Enforcement Authorities, 1943–1996," Prepared for the Attorney General of British Columbia, August 31, 1996.

Chapter 9: Marguerite Telesford—A Morning Jog Ends in Tragedy

Gordon Head News, April 12–18, 1988.
Victoria Times-Colonist, January 23, 26, 27, 31, 1989.

Chapter 10: The Unsolved Murder of Lindsay Buziak

Saanich Police Department
Victoria Times-Colonist, February 1, 2010.

Chapter 11: The Highway of Tears

Hiway 16 magazine
www.wikipedia.org/wiki/british_columbia_highway 16

Chapter 12: A Rediscovered Feng Shui Site

Castle, Geoffrey (ed.). *Saanich: An Illustrated History,* Saanich, BC: The Corporation of the District of Saanich, 1989.
Saanich News

Chapter 13: Woman from the Mist Performs a Miracle

Personal interview with Marguerite West, 1993.

Chapter 14: Five Marine Mysteries

Rogers, Fred. *More Shipwrecks of British Columbia*. Vancouver, BC: Douglas & McIntyre, 1992.
www.en.wikipedia.org/wiki/Graveyard_of_the_Pacific
www.marinemysteries.ca/site/mysteries.html
www.wikipedia.org/wiki/SS_Valencia

Chapter 15: The Changing Chilliwack Painting

Personal interview with Hetty Fredrickson, 1987.

Chapter 16: The Michael Dunahee Story

The Globe & Mail, August 10, 2006.

Personal correspondence and interviews with Crystal Dunahee, July 2011.

Victoria Police Department

Victoria Times-Colonist, March 1991.

www.en.wikipedia.org/wiki/Michael Dunahee

www.michaeldunahee.ca

Chapter 17: Monster Sightings—Ogopogo and Caddy

Bousefield, Edward L., and Paul H. LeBlond. *Cadborosaurus: Survivor from the Deep.* Surrey, BC: Heritage House Publishing, 2000.

Gaal, Arlene. *Ogopogo: The True Story of the Okanagan Lake Million Dollar Monster.* Surrey, BC: Hancock House, 1986.

Jupp, Ursula. *Cadboro: A Ship, a Bay, a Sea-Monster.* Victoria, BC: Jay Editions, 1988.

Victoria Daily Times, Summer 1930.

Victoria Times-Colonist, August 9, 1997; July 20, 2011.

Chapter 18: Sasquatch—Man or Beast?

www.bcscc.ca/sasquatch.htm

www.cbc.ca

www.en.wikipedia.org/wiki/Bigfoot

Chapter 19: Is There a UFO Triangle in BC?

The Interior News, Smithers, BC, November 18, 2004.

www.en.wikipedia.org/wiki/UFO_sightings_in_Canada

Chapter 20: Vancouver Island Hauntings

Adams, John. *Ghosts and Legends of Bastion Square.* Victoria, BC: Discover the Past, 2002.

Green, Valerie. *If These Walls Could Talk.* Victoria, BC: Touchwood Editions, 2001.

———. *If More Walls Could Talk.* Victoria, BC: Touchwood Editions, 2004.

Chapter 21: The Cariboo Camels

Fowler, Harlan Davey. *Three Caravans to Yuma: The Untold Story of Bactrian Camels in Western America.* Glendale, CA: Arthur H. Clark Publisher, 1980.

Stewart, John, assistant archivist, Kamloops Museum. *The Cariboo Camels.*

Chapter 22: Some Provincial Folklore

BC Folklore Society, www.folklore.bc.ca

Chapter 23: The Legend of Christmas Hill

Downs, Art, and Bruce Ramsey. Pioneer Days in British Columbia, Vancouver, BC: Fitzhenry & Whiteside, May 2002.

Green, Valerie. *Legends, Liars & Lawbreakers: Incredible Tales from the Pacific Northwest.* Canmore, AB: Altitude Publishing, 2004.

Saanich News, December 2, 1998.

Additional Sources

Kelowna Archives and Museum

Penticton Museum and Archives

Royal British Columbia Museum Archives

Saanich Archives

Saanich Police Archives

University of British Columbia Archives

Vancouver Archives

Victoria City Archives

Victoria City Police Archives

Valerie Green

Valerie Green was born and educated in England. She has a background in journalism and English literature. Among her many jobs, while freelancing on the side, she worked for a time at MI5 in London. She came to Canada in 1968. What was planned as a temporary move became permanent when she met her future husband two months into her stay. Valerie has authored 13 books, most dealing with British Columbia history, and she has contributed to many newspapers and magazines in the province. When not writing, she enjoys travel, photography, walking and the arts (especially theatre). She lives in Victoria with her husband.